GW00738544

Amazon Echo Spot

The Complete User Guide:
Learn to Use Your Echo Spot Like A Pro

by C.J. Andersen

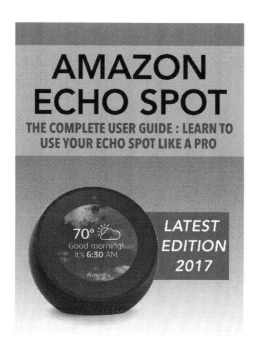

AMAZON ECHO SPOT
THE COMPLETE USER GUIDE : LEARN TO USE YOUR ECHO SPOT LIKE A PRO

LATEST EDITION 2017

Copyright © 2017 by CJ Andersen — All rights reserved.

AMAZON ECHO Spot is a trademark of Amazon Technologies Inc. All other copyrights & trademarks are the properties of their respective owners. Reproduction of any part of this book without the permission of the copyright owners is illegal — the only exception to this is the inclusion of brief quotes in a review of the work. Any request for permission should be directed to cjandersentech@gmail.com

Alexa Enabled Amazon Devices

Echo   Echo Plus

Echo Dot

Fire Tablets

Fire TV

Amazon Tap

Contents

Introduction

Hello and welcome! Thank you for buying this Echo Spot user guide and I look forward to sharing my knowledge and helping you to master your new Amazon device. If this is your first Amazon/Echo device then you will discover that the Alexa App is at the heart of everything you can do with the Echo Spot.

So, before we get under way I would like to make a couple of suggestions. Firstly, I would like to encourage you to sign up to my monthly Alexa Updates Newsletter and here's why... Amazon is constantly tweaking, updating and expanding the capabilities of both its devices (Fire tablets, Fire TV, Echo, Echo Show, Echo Spot etc) and its AI software Alexa.

And when I say constantly I mean ALL the time.

The Echo Spot has only been available for a few weeks and there have already been a number of improvements and noteworthy additions in the time it has taken me to write this guide. While I will continue to publish updated editions of this guide, I want to be sure that anyone who has bought this book has the chance to stay up to date with the frequent changes.

My Alexa Updates Newsletter is the solution. Once a month I will send out a roundup of any significant or newsworthy developments that will enhance the use of your Alexa enabled Amazon device...including the Echo Spot.

Of course you can unsubscribe from the newsletter at any time and I will never share your personal information with anyone. So go ahead and **Subscribe Today** at www.about.me/cjandersen.

Secondly, I wanted to say a word about this guide, how it has been put together and the best way to use it. Of course, you should feel free to go straight to a particular chapter if there is some specific information you are looking for, but I would also urge you to read the book in its entirety as it follows a logical progression.

For that reason I have laid out this guide to take you step by step from setting up your Echo Spot ready to start using and then through every option within the Alexa App starting at the top and working down to the bottom. It's really the easiest way to approach and master Alexa without jumping back and forth and getting lost in the numerous options.

I'll also be reviewing the many third-party apps and Alexa Skills that you can access via the Echo Spot to maximize your enjoyment of the device, including:

- Using music apps such as Amazon Music, Spotify, Tunein and iHeartRadio

- Linking up to audiobook services like Audible and Kindle

- Watching videos and movie trailers on the Spot

- Setting up the Spot as an integral part of your Smart Home technology

- Getting the most of the Alexa personal assistant, from setting alarms to ordering pizzas!

- And, of course, troubleshooting common glitches that crop up from time to time...

I am confident that anyone, no matter what level their tech skills, will find learning and using their Amazon Echo Spot pretty straight forward. If there's anything that you still find confusing after having read this guide then please email me at cjandersentech@gmail.com

Okay, let's go!

Before we get started: Echo Spot Basics

As an enthusiastic user of both the Amazon Echo and the Echo Show, I was super excited when the Spot was launched and have been very happy with its performance. The Spot is, to my mind, the perfect merger of the Echo's personal assistant capabilities with the added benefit of having the Show's screen for useful visual information (albeit a much smaller one); plus it works great as a really good-looking digital alarm clock!

The Spot has taken Echo's old place in the bedroom where I can:

- Set alarms and daily reminders
- Look at the weather forecast
- Listen to music while I'm getting dressed
- Get news flash briefings and traffic reports

- Drop in on the kids room to see that they're OK
- Make use of all the other benefits this personal assistant offers

One of the things I like best is that most of the information requested from Echo Spot also shows up on the Alexa App (more later), so I can view it there immediately or later when I want to review it.

I also like that if I unplug and move the Echo Spot, the device takes just a minute or two to reboot and reconnect to Wi-Fi.

A quick note on the wake word: Echo Spot requires a wake word to activate your device. For example, "Alexa, what's the weather like today" where "Alexa" is your wake word. I'm guessing you already know that, so in this guide I don't include a wake word when suggesting what to say to Alexa. For any voice command you read in this guide be sure to use your wake word first.

The Echo Spot Preview

Getting started with Echo Spot takes just a few minutes, and most of the setup happens automatically. Before you plug it in, though, look over your new Spot to familiarize yourself with the physical features of the hardware and the purpose of each.

On/Off, Mic & Camera Button: There are three buttons on the top of the device. This information is about the middle button as the Spot faces you:

- **On:** To turn on the device, press and hold the button for about three seconds. The Echo logo will appear shortly to let you know the device is on.

- **Disable Mic and Camera:** Press and quickly release this button to turn off the mic and camera so that Alexa won't "hear" the wake word and the camera no longer functions. However it is worth noting that even when these functions are disabled, you can still communicate with the device using the Alexa Voice Remote, a handy tool that is sold separately and discussed in the next chapter.

- **Off:** To turn off Echo Spot, press the button and hold slightly longer.

Volume Buttons: The left button (-) turns the volume down; the right button (+) turns it up. The level shows on the screen as you push the buttons, and there's a cute chirping sound when you adjust the volume.

Camera: The camera is in front, within the black ring that surrounds the screen.

Touch Screen: The round touch screen measures 2.5" in diameter can be used for many Echo Spot functions including turning off alarms, browsing entertainment or controlling music playback.

Light circle: The LED light circle extends around the whole of the screen and gives a variety of indications:

- **Blue and green intermingled:** Alexa is listening.

- **Blue:** Alexa is processing your request.

- **Orange:** Echo Spot is having Wi-Fi connectivity issues (See Troubleshooting for details on trouble connecting to Wi-Fi).

- **No lights:** If Echo Spot is on and the light bar is off, the device is ready and waiting.

Power supply and port: The power supply plugs into the back of the device near the bottom.

Audio port: There is a 3.5mm audio port next to the power port where you can connect headphones or speakers. They are not provided with the Spot.

Specifications of the Amazon Echo Spot

In case you're wondering, here are the specs of the device in front of you.

Dimensions and Weight:

- Height: 3.8 inches

- Width: 4.1 inches

- Base depth: 3.6 inches

- Weight: 14.8 ounces

Screen: 2.5" diameter

Audio: Built-in speaker and 3.5mm stereo audio output for use with external speakers (not included)

Processor: Intel Atom

Networking:

- Wireless

- 802.11a/b/g/n, Bluetooth wireless protocol

- Dual-band (2.4 GHz and 5 GHz)

- For security reasons, Echo Spot does not connect to ad-hoc or peer-to-peer networks

Warranty: 1 year

Echo Spot Hardware Accessories: at the time of writing there were no useful accessories for the Spot, but it will likely only be a matter of time before manufacturers see options for screen protectors and stands. It's worth noting though that the Spot has a specially designed rubber base to ensure that it doesn't slide off your nightstand that easily.

Echo Spot Vs Echo Show

Perhaps you're wondering whether the Echo Spot was the right purchase or if you'd have been happier with the Echo Show. I've got both, enjoy both, and find that both have pros and cons depending on how you use them.

The Echo Spot and Echo Show have much in common including that neither are portable, both run off a plug-in power adapter and they have the same Wi-Fi protocol and data link protocol.

Both have these capabilities:

- Bluetooth audio input

- Bluetooth audio output

- Compatibility with Alexa Voice Remote

- Broad personal assistant capabilities through Alexa (lists, timers, alarms, reminders, calendars, notifications, control smart home devices etc.)

- Media services like Amazon Music, Spotify and iHeartRadio

Neither device has:

- Media storage

- The Alexa Voice Remote included

Now, here's how Echo Spot is different than Echo Show:

- Echo Spot has a much smaller screen at 2.5" diameter compared to the Echo Show which has a 7" color screen

- Echo Spot has one small speaker (mono); Echo Show has two (stereo) and has Dolby audio

- Echo Spot has the possibility of connecting a speaker or headphone, whilst the Show does not have this option

On the face of it, you might say the Echo Show wins, and it's true that I have found the larger Echo Show screen to be a definite plus when seeing is better than hearing - shopping on Amazon, watching videos or reviewing my To-do list – and for listening to music at high volume.

But the Echo Spot is much more compact and is an ideal addition to my bedroom furnishings, where it functions primarily as digital alarm clock, with the added benefits of all the Alexa skills and functions should I need them (the weather report and reminders being particularly useful first thing in the morning). I also like that I can use the Spot to drop in on the kids' rooms to check how they're doing.

The Echo Show, I have found, is much better suited to sit on my breakfast bar where I can make better use of the larger screen whilst I'm preparing my food or eating.

Note on the Echo Spot sound: With its compact size, comes a tiny 1.4" speaker, so the Echo Spot is clearly not designed for entertaining a huge party with your entire music collection. The sound quality is fine though for listening to the flash news briefings and for conducting voice calls.

1: Let's Begin! — Echo Spot Setup

For any voice command you read in this chapter be sure to use your wake word ("Alexa", "Amazon", etc) first.

Setting up Echo Spot is largely an automated process once you plug in the device. Here's what should have come in the box:

- Echo Spot
- Power adapter with 6' cord
- Echo Spot startup guide
- Echo Spot "Things to Try" card

The protective film over the screen can be removed by pulling the tabs.

CJ's Tips: My Spot has a permanent spot on my nightstand. Perhaps try several locations to determine where you get maximum usage from your Echo Spot, and of course you may find that you move it occasionally. Wherever you place the device, Amazon recommends it is not placed too close to walls and windows, so that indoor echoes and outdoor noises don't confuse poor Alexa!

OK, enough with the preliminaries. Let's get the Spot started. Have your Wi-Fi password and your Amazon login information available for connection and setup.

1. Download the Alexa App to your phone and/or tablet (or see 5: below if you don't have a mobile device)

Mobile device requirements are:

- FireOS 3.0 or higher

- Android 5.0 or higher
- iOS 9.0 or higher

The quickest method for downloading the app is to go to the app store on your mobile device, look up the Alexa App and install it.

Once the Alexa App is installed, you will be able to access it on your mobile device and at alexa.amazon.com on your PC or Mac. It's a good idea to locate **Settings** on the App, because they are referred to often.

2: Plug in/Turn on Echo Spot

Plug the adapter into Echo Spot and an outlet, and the device will turn on.

3: Connect your Echo Spot to a Wi-Fi Network

Follow the prompts on your Echo Spot screen to choose the Wi-Fi network you select from a list of those available. You may be required to enter your Wi-Fi password at this point.

- If your network isn't on the list, you can add it by selecting **Add a Network** or **Rescan**.
- If you have been asked to enter a password, you will also be offered the option to save it to Amazon. This will help you if you go on to add more Echo devices to the same Wi-Fi network as the Wi-Fi password will automatically appear during Wi-Fi setup.
- Select **Connect** and your Spot should confirm its connection to your Wi-Fi network.

Connection trouble: If in the unlikely event that your Echo Spot does not connect to Wi-Fi, try these troubleshooting and solution tips in this order:

- Make sure your Wi-Fi is on
- Use another Wi-Fi device such as a tablet or computer to ensure Wi-Fi is working
- Tap the network you want to connect to and select the **Forget** option to reset the connection

- Attempt to connect to the network

- Make sure your network password (different than your Amazon password) is correct, and retry it

- If you saved your Wi-Fi password to Amazon but later changed it, you'll need to update the information on Amazon

- Turn off other devices connected to Wi-Fi; they might be causing too much congestion on the network for the Echo Spot to connect

- Move your Echo Spot away from a baby monitor or microwave oven that might be causing interference

- Try to connect to your router's 5GHz Wi-Fi frequency, if one is available, since that band might be less congested

Intermittent Wi-Fi: Sometimes an interruption in Wi-Fi prevents a connection. If your Wi-Fi goes out for brief periods, try this:

- Turn off the network hardware (router and separate modem if there is one)

- Wait 20-30 seconds

- Turn the modem on

- Turn the router on, if separate

- Unplug the Echo Spot, and plug it in again after three seconds

- Attempt the connection to Wi-Fi again

If nothing works, contact your Internet provider or router manufacturer.

If your network has an administrator, they might be able to help too.

4: Pair mobile devices with Echo Spot

I recommend taking this step now since you're in a Startup frame of mind. This is a separate function from downloading the App to your device and using Echo Spot from there. Since Echo Spot is Bluetooth-enabled, you can use it as a standalone Bluetooth speaker to stream your favorite audio services from your tablet or phone. This is particularly important if you predominately use Google Play Music and iTunes on your mobiles.

- Go to your phone's or other device's Settings and select Bluetooth to ensure that Bluetooth is On.

- Say, "Pair my phone" or "pair my tablet," or go to **Settings** on the Alexa App, select Echo Spot and then follow the prompts for **Bluetooth > Pair a New Device**, and pairing will occur.

- Alexa will say, "Connected to _____ phone".

- Your device's Bluetooth Settings should list your Echo Spot when the two are paired.

- Say, "Cancel," to stop Bluetooth pairing if you want to exit the mode before connection, and say "Disconnect" when you want to disconnect your mobile device from the Echo Spot.

CJ's Tips: You can only connect the Echo Spot with one mobile device at a time. It will automatically connect to the most recently paired device. So to change to a different device by Bluetooth, you will need to first disconnect the current device that is paired, by saying, "Disconnect" and then connect the new device following the above instructions.

5: Access the Alexa App on your computer, and sign in (optional)

This is my preferred way to use the App, followed by using my tablet and finally the phone. I like the larger view. The App address is: alexa. amazon.com

6: Customize the Echo Spot device home screen and sounds

I suggest you wait a few days or a week before customizing the device home screen to see how you like default mode, but the information is included here as part of the general setup process.

- Go to **Settings**, you can either do this via the Alexa App on your computer, or by tapping the touch screen with your fingers or by saying "Go to Settings".

- Choose or tap the option for **Home Screen.**

- Choose or tap **Background** to change the background from Default to a photo uploaded from your phone via the Alexa App or one from your Prime Photos collection.

- Use the Back arrow to go back to the Home Screen settings, and choose **Home Card Preferences** to choose whether things like Notifications, Reminders or Calendar appear on your screen and how often they appear.

- From the **Settings** page, tap **Display** to customize the screen more comprehensively with easy-to-follow prompts.

- For choosing sounds preferences, go to the device's **Settings**, tap **Sounds** and choose levels for Media volume and Alarm, Timer and Notification Volume before browsing Custom Sounds.

CJ's Tips: There are two other solutions when Echo Spot's screen is distracting you — turn it away from you or say, "Turn off your screen." With the voice command, the screen will go dark until you tap it or make a new request.

7: Create an Amazon Household

This is another setup feature you might want to wait till later to do, if at all.

If there are other Amazonians in your household — your literal or figurative "household" — you might want to share capabilities such as being able to listen to each other's music. You can explore the benefits and how-to's of Amazon Households in more detail by following the instructions below or going to www.amazon.com/myh/manage.

- On Amazon.com hover over **Accounts & Lists** near the top of the page

- Select "Your Account"

- In the "Shopping programs and rentals" box (bottom right), select **Amazon Households** to go to the Manage Your Household / Your Amazon Household Benefits page

- Select "Add an Adult," and follow the instructions including providing their login information, so they will have to give it to you or be there with you to type it in

- And/or select "Add a Child," Create and Save their Profile, and follow the link to Manage Your Content and Devices to determine the content they can access

8: Set up the Alexa voice remote (optional)

The Alexa voice remote is available on Amazon for $29.99 (www.amzn. to/2v4e9Q8). Its availability has been intermittent, though at this writing, it is in stock.

Be aware that there is also an Alexa voice remote for Amazon Fire TV and Fire TV Stick. That's not what you want here. While Echo Spot is equipped with Far-field voice recognition to pick up the wake word and queries, there are times the remote is a handy alternative to talking across the room, especially when there is other noise in the space that will cause you to shout or that will confuse Alexa.

Once the remote's batteries are installed, it might pair automatically. This has been hit and miss with users. If it doesn't, you can pair it via the Alexa App.

Pair the remote using the app by going to **Settings**; select your device (your Echo Spot); select **Pair Remote**.

2: Meet the Alexa App

For any voice command you read in this chapter be sure to use your wake word ("Alexa", "Amazon", etc) first.

Now that Setup is complete, you'll get the most utility from the Echo Spot and complete tasks more quickly if you know your way around the Alexa App. We will refer to **Settings** several times here. They are a part of the App, but there's so much information to share about **Settings** that it has its own chapter (page 100). It's inevitable that some information will be covered in both places.

Amazon calls Alexa the "brain behind" its Echo devices. Alexa is cloud-based, making it possible for Alexa and Echo Spot to continually be improved and updated. If you're worried about security, consider that it's likely that many of your accounts are already somewhere in the cloud — banking, credit cards, medical in addition to other Amazon accounts such as Prime or Drive. The same level of security used with that information is used with Alexa.

The App, your Voice and the Screen

Most of what you can do via the Alexa App can also be done with voice. If you're listening to an Amazon music station, for example, you can select the Pause button on the App or simply say, "pause." In the remainder of this guide, we will note things you cannot do by voice, such as Change the Wake Word. In all other cases, assume you can accomplish the task with your voice, and give it a try.

There is also interplay between the App and the Spot's touch screen. For example, when you're listening to media, the **Now Playing** page will display on the Echo Spot screen, and when you add an item to your **Shopping List**, the list will appear for about 30 seconds before the screen reverts to its Default display. The display can be customized in

Settings on the App and on the Echo Spot device.

Note on clarifying terms: In tech talk about devices, the terms "page" and "screen" are sometimes used interchangeably in a confusing manner. To be clear, in this guide, a "page" is a page on the App you can view on your phone, tablet or computer; the "screen" is the Echo Spot device touch screen.

A Word about Help & Feedback

The *Help & Feedback* page, accessible within the Alexa App, is discussed in detail later, but it's worth knowing before we get started that this section contains a wealth of information about all the topics discussed throughout the rest of this book.

Alexa App Home Page

As you view the App layout at Alexa.Amazon.com, you'll see a Menu of App pages on the left and the current page on the right. That's what you might see on large mobile devices too, but on most phones and tablets, you will see just the current page. The Menu will be depicted with three horizontal lines.

Now, let's explore the Home page, starting at the top. It includes Things to Try, your Cards and, when you're playing most media, a music player.

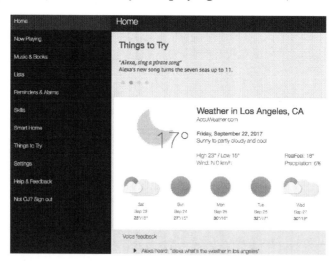

Things to Try: When on the *Home* page, a Things to Try feature appears at the very top. It rotates through some suggestions of things to say to Alexa related to current or trending issues.

There are shaded buttons below the suggestions. I click manually through them since I don't have the patience to watch them rotate at the rate of 7–8 seconds per suggestion. Occasionally something of interest appears, like Brain Facts — Learn something new about the human brain — but I've found they can be a time waster in the same way social media can be when there are other things I should be doing.

Cards: The next things you'll see after the Things to Try suggestions are your Cards. A Card is created with most verbal interactions with Alexa. The Card preserves the request and response from Alexa such as a music station or a forecast you requested, a recipe you've selected, a Skill used or items you added to your shopping list.

Cards form your Alexa Dialog History. You can scroll down the Cards to review them. A list of them is also available in Settings. Select *Settings*, and scroll down to the *General* section, and select *History*.

Card options: On the right of each Card you'll see the word More with a V-shaped icon, known as a caret. Click on it to see options for further action:

- **Remove card:** Select this to delete the card

- **Give Voice feedback:** The Card will show what "Alexa heard" with the question, "Did Alexa do what you wanted?" Answering the question helps Alexa improve its understanding of how you speak. You don't have to answer the question, of course. If you answer "no," you'll be given the option to "Send more detailed feedback". Select that for unlimited space to provide feedback and the opportunity to request that Amazon get back to you on your input.

Learn More: This takes you to Alexa and Alexa Device FAQs, which is a useful part of the *Help & Feedback* section of the menu I recommend you browse when you have a few minutes.

Deleting your entire history at once is only possible by deregistering your device, something you'd likely do only if giving it away or selling it. Deregistering the Echo Spot and reregistering it is explained in the **Settings** section.

Bing Search and Wikipedia: One or both these options might appear on a Card:

- **Search Bing:** If Alexa is unclear about what you say or if you ask about a person, place or thing, Alexa will provide the option to "Search Bing for..." whatever your query was about. Bing is your only search engine option on the App.

- **Learn more on Wikipedia:** Depending on the subject you ask Alexa about, the Card might give you a short answer and a link to the topic on Wikipedia.

Player: When media (songs, radio, podcasts, etc.) is loaded, whether playing or paused, the Player appears at the bottom of the Alexa app page and allows you to control it. The bar includes an icon of the current song in the queue. The Player appears at the bottom of the App regardless of what page you're on when viewing the App on a PC or Mac. It is discussed fully in the **Now Playing** section next.

3: The 'Now Playing' Page and Player

For any voice command you read in this chapter be sure to use your wake word ("Alexa", "Amazon", etc) first.

One of Alexa's most attractive features is its ability to play media from a wide range of sources. Those platforms are explored in detail in the next chapter: **Music, Videos & Books**. There, we'll also discuss how to make a request for specific music or a general request such as, "Play Acoustic Indie music."

I appreciate that you might not yet have anything to play yet and therefore much of this chapter might not make sense to you yet. If this is the case feel free to skip ahead and return to this chapter when you are ready.

For most of your audio content, the ***Now Playing*** page displays an icon for the source such as iHeartRadio, Kindle audiobooks or a podcast on Tunein to remind you where the media is coming from.

You can manually click any option on the Now Playing page or you can use voice.

The player always offers these control symbols:

- **Play/Pause:** Manually select or say, "Pause," "Resume," "Play" or "Stop."

- **Go back:** Manually select or say, "Go back."

- **Go forward:** Manually select or say, "Go forward."

- **Sound level vertical slide:** Slide the volume bar manually by "grabbing" it or use a verbal command such as "volume seven" or "mute."

- **Song progress bar:** When using the App on a computer, selecting a place earlier or later in the song isn't possible. Ability to change the place in the song varies on mobile devices.

Depending on what type of audio you are playing, additional options are shown on the player:

- **Thumb Up & Thumb Down:** Rate the song, and Alexa will use your opinion to tailor your music stations to your preferences

- **Shuffle:** Selecting the crossed arrows will cause the Queue to be played in random order

- **Repeat:** Select the looping arrows to repeat the song or station when it is completed

In the upper right of the ***Now Playing*** page are two lists you can view **Queue** and **History** by selecting your choice.

Queue: This is the list of selections in the media you've chosen such as the Classical Focus Prime Station I'm currently enjoying. Expand your options for each piece by selecting the V-shaped caret. For music, expanding the box allows you to choose further actions like:

- Rate the song by choosing Thumb Up or Thumb Down.

- Shop the Digital Music Store, which will open in a new page with the standard features seen on all Amazon product pages.

- View album in Prime Music, if applicable, which will open in a page that looks very much like the Digital Store page but with the opportunity to buy any/all the songs on the recording.

- When listening to podcasts or radio stations, clicking the caret and expanding the box allows you to mark what you're listening to as a Favorite program.

History: This is the list of media you've played from all sources.

Play anything from Queue or History by tapping/clicking it. Your choice will then become the audio content that is ***Now Playing***.

CJ's Tips: Note that if you are playing a station and then select another media, the station might be canceled. I learned this by pausing a station and asking for my news **Flash Briefing** (explained later but found in ***Settings*** if you want to explore it before we get to it). The station did not resume, even at my request. Stations are not canceled if you ask for your weather forecast, something from Wikipedia or a simple question. The station volume is reduced while Alexa fulfills the request. I'm still learning which requests cancel stations and which don't. If a station gets canceled, and I want to continue listening, it's right there in History where I can pick up where I left off.

Now Playing on the Echo Spot Screen

Most media will appear on the Echo Spot screen too, but the Player control options might be more limited. Tap the screen to see the player, and tap the appropriate control to pause, play, go back or forward one song, drag the song to the end, shuffle the songs or repeat.

As mentioned above, if any of this is confusing right now then read on and return to this chapter once you have started playing some audio.

4: Watch This and More! — Video

For any voice command you read in this chapter be sure to use your wake word ("Alexa", "Amazon", etc) first.

Video is the first section listed in the App's **Music, Video & Books** section, so that's where we will begin. The section's title covers a lot of ground and still doesn't fully capture all that's available here. Video is new to the Echo universe with the introduction of the Echo Show, and it is now available - albeit in a much smaller format - on the Echo Spot. Consequently, you might not really use the Spot for watching video, but it's worth reviewing what video services are available via the Alexa App and how to access them. Music options for the Echo devices of course continue to grow, and the Books platforms, Kindle for eBooks (Amazon simply refers to them as Books now) and Audible for audiobooks, have their enthusiastic users too.

Let's take the list of services on this page from top to bottom. Since Amazon continues to update what's available, the list might change, as it did while writing this book, and be different when you're reading it. The good news is that each service sets up very easily.

The basic idea for all the services is that you establish an account with the service and then link Alexa/Echo Spot to it.

At this writing, Alexa Video supports Fire TV and Dish TV, though Amazon reports it is "working hard to bring additional services to Alexa."

Watch Amazon Video on Echo Spot

Personally I don't watch content from Amazon Video on my Spot, the screen is just too small, but it can be done!

Amazon Video is a huge offering of digital movies and TV shows you can watch on Echo Spot by simply asking for a title. The media can also be watched on computers, Amazon Fire devices, iOS and Android devices, TVs and more. Let's talk about Amazon Video on Echo Spot.

Video can be obtained from three sources:

Amazon Video: Digital versions of movies, TV shows and series and any other video content that you've purchased individually from Amazon to form your Video Library.

Amazon Prime Membership and Prime for Students: Thousands of video titles for movies, TV shows and Amazon original content are available at no additional cost with a Prime trial or membership. To see what's on offer go to the Amazon Video department (www.amzn. to/2xoFa2Q) on the Amazon website and click the tab that says *Included with Prime*.

Video Subscriptions: Hundreds of premium third-party channels like HBO, Starz and Showtime plus many for kids and other niche genres are not free with Prime but can be subscribed to individually from the Amazon website. To see these third party services again go to the Amazon Video page and this time click the Channels tab.

Join Amazon Prime by selecting *Try Prime* near the top left of any Amazon page.

Watch Video on Echo Spot: Once you've got something to watch, there are many ways you can access it.

- **Search your library:** Say "Show me my video library" or "Show me my watchlist," and it will appear on the screen where you can browse by swiping left and tapping what you want to watch.

- **Search by title:** Say "Show me [specific movie or show title]", and it will play.

- **Show by actor or genre:** Say, "Show me Harrison Ford movies," or "Show me animated movies," and search results you can browse will appear on the screen.

Alexa will reply, "Here's what I found," to all these requests as the results appear.

Once the content is being shown, you can control it in two ways:

- Tap the screen to view and use the limited player that includes pause/play and symbols for going back or forward 10 seconds.

- Use voice with common commands including: "Play/pause/resume", "Rewind/fast forward", "Go back/skip ahead and number of seconds, minutes or hours", "Next video/next episode".

Watch Movie Trailers on Echo Spot

You can watch any move trailer from IMDB on Echo Spot by simply asking. Say, "Show me the movie trailer for [movie title]."

You can control the trailer playback two ways:

- Tap the screen to view and use the limited player that includes pause/play and symbols for going back or forward 10 seconds

- Use voice with common commands, such as "Play", "Pause" etc.

CJ's Tips: I quite like using my Echo Spot to watch movie trailers, they are exactly the kind of short video content that work really well on the small screen. I'm not convinced there's much value in being able to play the rest of my Amazon Video Library on the Spot, as I'd far prefer to view most TV series and movies on a bigger screen like my TV. In fact that brings us neatly to Amazon's Fire TV. Using the Alexa App to operate your Fire TV is definitely useful!

Fire TV

This Amazon product line is a comprehensive TV media and personal assistant center that can be paired with and controlled by any Echo device. But to be clear, if you would like to use Fire TV with your Echo Spot you will need to buy one of the Fire TV device options.

What you can watch with Fire TV: Most streaming and live TV services can be viewed with Fire TV including: Netflix, Hulu, HBO Now, Crackle, Amazon, ESPN, Showtime, Sling, DirectTV Now, NBA, MLB. TV, CNN, Comedy Central, HGTV and AMC.

What else you can do with Fire TV and Alexa: Enjoy music services played through your equipment such as Amazon Music, and iHeartRadio, order pizza or an Uber, browse Yelp and play games from developers like EA and Disney. Search "Fire TV" on Amazon to see everything the service offers.

Connecting Alexa and Fire TV: Amazon provides complete instructions for setting up Fire TV equipment and a PDF Users Guide to make the most of Fire TV. To control Fire TV with Alexa:

- Go to *Music, Video & Books* in the Alexa App, and select *Fire TV*

- Select *Link Your Alexa Device*

- Select the device you want to link

- Follow the onscreen prompts to complete linking of Alexa to the Fire TV Player

Once setup is complete, put Alexa to work with requests like:

- "Watch House of Cards"

- "Next episode"

- "Rewind 10 minutes"

- "Jump to 30 minutes"

- "Show me Emma Watson movies"

- "Play Sia music"

- "Order Domino's pizza"

And literally thousands of other requests. To be clear, linking your Alexa enabled device like the Echo Spot will allow you to control your Fire TV options on your big screen TV set. (Great for watching movies in bed!)

Dish TV

This television service appeals mostly to those that have already subscribed to a Dish TV package (www.dish.com/programming/packages), which currently starts at $49.99/month plus $10/month for the Hopper DVR. Dish TV has pushed its Alexa relationship by periodically offering new customers an Amazon Echo Dot upon signup. You can check the availability of this offer at www.dish.com.

Required: Dish TV Package, DISH Hopper Smart DVR

Devices currently supported: Hopper 3 and newer, Hopper with Sling, Hopper and Wally

Benefits: Play Dish TV via Echo Spot, and ask Alexa to:

- Change the channel (ex. "Go to channel 75")
- Search for shows, movies or actors (ex. "Find Modern Family on Dish" — Alexa will look for options on the services you have such as Netflix, Hulu and Amazon Prime)
- Play your recorded content (ex. "Play Dallas Cowboys football game")
- Pause, fast-forward and rewind what's being shown (ex. "Rewind 2 minutes")

Setting Up Dish TV on Alexa:

- Go to *Music, Videos & Books*
- Select *Dish TV*
- Enable the Skill
- Have your Dish TV and Amazon login information handy, since you might need to enter it during setup. Follow the on-screen instructions to connect Alexa to Dish TV which include: 1.) Turning on your Hopper setup box and TV 2.) Enter the code given on the TV screen into the Alexa App
- You might also need to update your Hopper's software to the latest version before you can use Dish TV with Alexa. On your Dish

set-top box, navigate to channel 9607 and locate/select "software update" to update your receiver to the latest software. Allow the software update to complete and the Hopper box to restart before returning to the Alexa app to attempt to link again

- Select **Finish Setup** in the Alexa app

- Follow on-screen prompts to link Echo Spot to the TV or other equipment you use to watch TV and other video services

If you have issues with the process, try these fixes:

Update the Alexa App, and make sure you signed into the App with the same account information you used to register your Echo Spot device — that is, make sure your App and device are on the same account. If not:

- Sign into the account the Echo Spot device is registered with, or

- Deregister the device and reregister it on the account you typically use.

To deregister your Echo Spot:

- Go to www.amazon.com/mycd

- Select **Your Devices**

- Select the box to the right of the appropriate device

- In the popup window, select **Deregister your device**

- Follow the onscreen prompts

If you continue to have issues linking Alexa with Dish TV then I suggest visiting www.dish.com/amazonalexaintegration for more information and/or contacting Dish TV directly.

A Word about YouTube

NB. At the start of October 2017 Google, the owners of YouTube, removed access to YouTube videos on Echo devices. I have left this section, about accessing YouTube content in this guide because I hope that Amazon and Google will come to some agreement in the near future.

Alexa and YouTube have a casual relationship at this point. There's no access to YouTube via an Alexa App page, just through voice requests.

Saying, "YouTube" will get no response from Alexa, as of this writing. Saying, "YouTube Jimmy Kimmel" or "YouTube How to fix a faucet" will bring the reply, "OK, this is what I found from YouTube," and a list of recent or popular videos will be displayed. Scroll through them by sliding left and selecting the one you want to watch. The more specific your request is, the more likely you are to get the video you want. You can restrict access to YouTube using the Echo Spot device Settings. Select ***Settings > Restrict Access > YouTube*** where you can block YouTube search or turn on Restricted Mode.

When watching a YouTube video, it will not appear on the Alexa App player. Tap the screen for a Player with limited controls or use basic voice controls. Note that if you pause a YouTube video and don't resume it within a few minutes, it will be gone. You'll have to request it again, and no Cards are generated by YouTube videos. Because of the popularity of YouTube and the power of Google, it's possible a more integrated relationship will evolve between Alexa and the world's top video sharing site...or not!

5: Songs by the Millions — Music

For any voice command you read in this chapter be sure to use your wake word ("Alexa", "Amazon", etc) first.

It's difficult to beat Alexa and the Echo devices for ease and convenience for playing music from a diverse range of sources. As you will see when you click/tap on **Music, Video & Books** within the Alexa App there are several further options under the heading. Let's look at each in order.

My Music Library

This section of the app is where you access YOUR personal music collection; the next section, **Amazon Music**, is where you can access ALL music available from Amazon. The order seemed logically backwards to me when **My Music Library** was sparse, but now that I have a large Library of music, it makes sense. I access what I already have more often than I want to browse what else is available.

Your account's My Music Library will be populated with music which has been:

- Imported: These are playlists you've uploaded to your Amazon Music account on Amazon.com from sources such as iTunes, Google Play and the Windows Media Player.

- Purchased from Amazon.

- Selected in the form of a Playlist from Amazon Prime and Amazon Music Unlimited subscriptions (discussed later).

To import music to your Music Library use your PC or Mac and follow these steps:

- Go to music.amazon.com/home and log in.

- Choose *Upload your music* from the left menu.

- Install the Amazon Music for PC/Mac App on your computer when prompted.

- Upload/import up to 250 songs to the Amazon cloud for free.

CJ's Tips: The Amazon Music app for your desktop computer is Amazon's equivalent of the iTunes app. Once you have it installed you can play all the music in you Amazon Music account on your PC or Mac just like you probably do on iTunes already.

And if you want to upload 250 songs for free from iTunes into Amazon Music then it's as simple as opening both apps and dragging music from iTunes into the *Upload Drag & drop here* box that you can find in the *right* menu bar of you Amazon Music app. Uploaded music will now appear in My Music Library on the Alexa app.

Optional: Get an Amazon Music storage subscription for $24.99/ year to import up to 250,000 songs by going to *Your Amazon Music*

Settings (www.amzn.to/2x8ukOX) in your Amazon account, scroll down to *Music Storage* and following the instructions from there.

While we're on the topic of Amazon Music subscriptions I think you'll enjoy having an Amazon Prime or Amazon Music Unlimited subscription, so here is a comparison of the two subscription options:

Amazon Prime including Amazon Music:

- Benefits: 2 million+ songs in Prime Music and a long list of shipping, shopping and media benefits that can be viewed on Amazon.

- Standard annual: $99/year after 30-day free trial

- Standard monthly: $10.99/month

- Student annual: $49 after free 6-month trial

Amazon Music Unlimited:

- Benefits: "Tens of millions of songs" according to Amazon.

- Echo Plan: $3.99/month after 30-day free trial — available with any Echo device including Spot.

There are individual and family plans for those without an Echo device too.

CJ's Tips: For what it's worth, my recommendation is getting a Prime membership since it offers so many other benefits, and then if you don't find enough of the kind of music you enjoy, consider a Music Unlimited subscription. Again you can manage all music subscriptions from here: www.amzn.to/2x8ukOX

So, now let's explore the **My Music Library** page from top to bottom.

Whose Device: The first option, if you have more than one Echo device, is to select the device you want to play music on.

Whose Library: Select the music Library you want to access. If you have set up an Amazon Household, you can access Libraries of household members too. An Amazon Household can include up to two adults, though each must have an Amazon account, and up to four children. Creating and managing an Amazon Household is done through your Amazon account on the Amazon.com website.

Here again are brief instructions and options.

- Hover over **Accounts & Lists** near the top of the page on Amazon. com

- Select **Your Account**

- In the **Shopping programs and rentals** box, select **Amazon Households** to go to the Manage Your Household / Your Amazon Household Benefits page

- Select **Add an Adult,** and follow the instructions including providing their login information, so they will have to give it to you or be there with you to type it in

- And/or select **Add a Child,** Create and Save their Profile, and follow the link to Manage Your Content and Devices to determine the content they can access

Here is a direct link: www.amazon.com/myh/manage

Search your library: Use the search box to find songs or albums more quickly in your Library. As you type the search word, a list of results will begin to populate and gradually narrow the more of the term you complete. Echo Spot is searching My Music Library only and will show a list very closely matching your search term or will return **No Results Found** if appropriate once you select **Enter.**

The next row is a menu of tabs: **Playlists / Artists / Albums / Songs / Genres**. Using them is a very straightforward process, so just a few comments will suffice for each.

Playlists: There are two sections here:

>Auto Playlists:

- **Imported** — These are playlists you've imported to Amazon Music account from your PC or Mac using the instructions above.

- **Purchased** — This is a list of all the songs you've purchased from Amazon, and in time it might become a very long and eclectic list.

- **Recently Added** — Just what it says — recently imported playlists and a list of songs purchased in the last month or so.

>Prime Playlists

If you don't have a Prime membership then you won't see anything here. If you do then it's time to add some to your Music Library!

More than 1,700 Amazon Music Playlists have been curated, and the number is growing. When you add a Playlist from those available with an Amazon Prime subscription, it will appear here in your **Prime Playlists** library. Browse Playlists at music.amazon.com/home or in your Amazon Music app. Hover over a list, and a + sign will appear. Select it to add the list to your **My Music Library**.

There are many ways to browse the Playlists on Amazon Prime and Music Unlimited. For example, on Prime, select the All Moods & Genres tab to view a drop-down menu. Scroll down the page to see Playlists that Amazon suggests for you based on your purchasing and listening history. The Top Playlists section includes trending lists, and Newly Released Playlists are just that.

Hover over or click on a Playlist to see your options:

- Select the + sign to add the entire list to your My Music Library "sight unseen," or later the X sign to remove it

- Choose the Play icon to listen to the list, or later, the Pause icon to pause it

- Select the three dots to:

  — Share the list: Copy the link, copy the page code to embed elsewhere, email the link or share it on Facebook or Twitter.

  — Follow the list by receiving updates when it is altered, and later Unfollow.

— Open the Playlist to view how long it is, number of songs in the list, who curated the list and what its reviews are. There, you can also tailor the list by adding only the songs from it that you want as part of the list.

Artists/Albums/Songs/Genres: These tabs all function the same, and you can find the music you want in two ways: Scroll down through the alphabetical list at the left or jump down to its location using the #ABCDEFG, etc., list. Of course, you can also ask Alexa to play the music you want.

CJ's Tips: In my experience, it helps to be as specific as possible when asking for music, such as, "Play Bruce Springsteen Born to Run from My Music Library," or "Play Bruce Springsteen Born to Run from Amazon Music." Once you have a few different music services set up it helps Alexa if you let her know exactly which service you want the music to come from. I will talk about setting Default Music Services later to make this process even easier.

Amazon Music

For this section to be relevant, you'll need a subscription to Amazon Prime and/or Amazon Music Unlimited. Here, you can explore all Stations and Playlists available through the services you subscribe to.

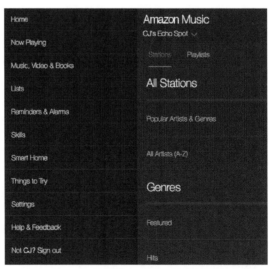

Stations: It's easy to find music in tune with your preferences.

- **All Stations:** This section has two categories to browse, and when you make a selection, the Station begins to play. Popular Genres & Artists stations include Classical Focus, Top Pop, Smooth Jazz, Lullabies & Bedtime Stories and other broad categories. Each of the All Artists (A-Z) stations brings together the very best music from across the band's or artist's career. Try this feature for yourself, of course, but I rarely use it. There is no search function, and scrolling down thousands of artists is impractical. There is a scroll bar on the right, though it's difficult to see since it is black on dark gray. However, the list is so large that it is difficult to scroll slowly enough to see each entry without skipping many.

- **Genres:** This is a more reasonable way to locate music you like, but you must go two levels deep to choose stations. Search categories including Featured, Pop, Country, Classic Rock, Christian, Alternative, Reggae, Clean, World, R&B, Classical and many more. When you do, you are given the list of subgenres. For example, choosing the Classical genre gives you the choice of dozens of stations like Baroque, Classical Piano, Classical Piano, etc., and popular artists like Yo-Yo Ma, the Emerson String Quartet and Hilary Hahn.

Playlists: I've already shown you (in the My Music Library section above) how to add playlists to your personal Music Library. Now here in your Amazon Music page you have the option to simply start searching and listening to other playlists. All available Playlists are currently categorized into four headings: Mood & Activities, Genres, Artists and Decade, and you must go to the second level to select a Playlist. Choose the category you're interested in, and then browse the Playlists available. Click the one you want, and it will begin to play.

The *Now Playing* page will show any Station or Playlist being played, and you can use all the Player, Queue and History features discussed earlier. My one complaint is that there is no scroll bar on the App, even when viewing it on a computer, to drag up or down to speed up finding what you want.

CJ's Tips: Here are a few tips and tricks to streamline the process of listening to your Amazon Music subscriptions.

Tip 1: Annoyingly you can't add a Prime Playlist to your Music Library via the App. However you can do it using your voice. First go to *Music, Video & Books > Amazon Music > Playlists* within the App and find a playlist you want to add. Click/tap the playlist to start it playing. Once it's playing you can then ask "Alexa, add this playlist to my library" and Alexa will do just that!

Tip 2: Every track you hear on a Prime Playlist or Station comes from an album that is also available for you to listen to free as a Prime member. However, adding an album to your Music Library requires a little bit of detective work.

Here's an example... you hear the song "Don't" by Ed Sheeran on a Prime Playlist and decide you would like to listen to the whole album that the song comes from.

First open up the Amazon Music app by going to music.amazon.com in the browser of your desktop computer.

Second search "Don't Ed Sheerin" in the search box at the top of the App page and hit enter.

Third, your results will be shown so scroll down to Prime Songs and when you see the song "Don't, Ed Sheeran" click the three vertical dots to the right of the track. A pop up window will appear giving you further options and one of those options should be *View Album*.

Fourth, go ahead and click *View Album* and you will be shown the entire album that the track is from *plus* the option to + *Add to My Music*, and clicking that will add the album (in this example the album is called "X (Wembley Edition)") to your music library.

Now you're all set and can just ask "Alexa, play the album X from my music library"

Tip 3: Once some music is playing via your Echo Spot you can control it with your voice with some pretty obvious commands like "Alexa...

what's this song", "...pause", "...turn down the volume", "...resume", "... next song", "...repeat this song" etc.

But did you know you can be a bit more adventurous than that? Try asking "Alexa, play dinner party music" or "Alexa, play music I can dance to" and see what Alexa comes up with!

Spotify

With 140 million users and 50 million subscribers, www.spotify.com is one of the largest music streaming platforms. While Spotify has a free subscription, a premium account is required for use with Echo Spot. That's Spotify's choice. The current cost of a premium account is $9.99/ month for those who have not tried Premium before. Besides using their service with the Echo Spot, benefits include the ability to download music to your devices to listen offline, skip songs you don't like as often as you want, play any song and listen without ads.

To create an account, choose an email address to link to, a password, user name and payment method, which can be a credit card or PayPal. If you choose PayPal, Spotify will connect to PayPal, and you might have to sign in. Once on PayPal, you will select which payment associated with your account you want to use.

Linking Alexa to Spotify: Once you have a premium account, select

Spotify from the *Music, Video & Books* tab, and choose:

Link your account > **Authorize the Account** (If asked)

A new window will open where you will have to authorize the connection of Alexa to your Spotify account. Once you do that, return to the Alexa App where you will be asked whether you want to make Spotify your default music service. If you want to change that later, it can be done at *Settings > Music & Media > Choose default music services*. There, you can select a Default music library and a Default station service.

If you want to unlink your Spotify account, for example if you no longer own the Echo Spot, select **Settings > *Music & Media* > *Spotify*** and ***Unlink Account from Alexa***. On that page, you can also go to Spotify to Manage Spotify Settings such as upgrade to a Premium for Family account, view and edit your profile or see when the next Renew date is.

Using Spotify on Echo Spot: If you've made Spotify your Default music service, you can use your voice or the Spotify app to play music from the service. For voice, simply request music from your favorite artist, and Alexa will play it. If it's not the Default service, you'll have to say, "Play Selena Gomez on Spotify," for example. As usual, the Player will appear on the Now Playing page and at the bottom of any other page you're viewing. Manually control Player functions using the Alexa App, with your voice – Play, Skip, Shuffle, etc., or on the Echo Spot screen.

CJ's Tips: I've mentioned Default Music Services a couple of times now so let's discuss them more fully. On the Alexa App go to ***Settings > Music & Media > Choose default music services***. Your current options (they may change) include setting a default music library (choosing between Amazon Music and Spotify) and a default station service (choose between Amazon Music, Pandora and iHeartRadio).

Once a default has been chosen Alexa will always search that service first when you make a request like "Alexa, play Avril Lavigne". Choose your preferred library and station service based on which sources you use the most, and remember that if you want music from a different source you will have to state that resource in your request, eg. "Alexa, play Avril Lavigne from iHeartRadio".

One quirk to watch out for, I have Amazon Music set as my default library and station service, but if I want to hear something from My Music Library I still have to specify it in my request and be really specific if I want a particular album. Example I asked Alexa "Play Earth, Wind & Fire" and, instead of tracks by the band Earth, Wind & Fire, Alexa started playing a track called "Earth, Wind and Fire" by Miguel from Prime music. I tried again "Alexa, play Earth, Wind & Fire from My Music Library" and things got better as Alexa played a range of the band's tracks from across My Music Library, but I specifically wanted to hear the Greatest Hits album so I had to try once more, "Alexa, play Earth, Wind & Fire Greatest Hits" before I got exactly what I wanted.

I just relay this fascinating anecdote to demonstrate that setting a default music service is still no substitute for getting into the habit of being as specific as possible with all your requests!

Pandora

You can use Alexa/Echo Spot with a free Pandora account, which I do. If you already have an account, you can skip to *Linking Alexa to Pandora* below.

There are currently three membership levels which you can find at www.pandora.com:

- **Pandora Free:** Free; Ad-supported radio; Personalized stations.
- **Pandora Plus:** $4.99/month; 30-day free trial; Ad-free Personalized stations; Better audio; Offline radio.
- **Pandora Premium:** $9.99/month; 60-day free trial; Ad-free; Create new stations and playlists rather than personalizing existing stations; Better audio; No limit on skips and replays; Download music to other devices.

Select the level you prefer, and you'll be taken to an account signup page. Even if you select a free trial for a paid subscription, providing an email address and password on the first page will immediately begin a free account.

Linking Alexa to Pandora: Back on the Alexa App, select **Pandora** from the *Music, Video & Books* page. Then, choose:

Link your account > Authorize the link

Using Pandora on Echo Spot: Once Alexa and Pandora are linked, you'll have two options on the Pandora page on the Alexa App.

- Choose + **Create Station,** and enter an artist, genre or track to search or scroll through the **Browse Genre** section to view more than 60 genres from standards like Rock, Alternative, Classical, Hip Hop/Rap, Instrumental, Comedy and Decades to niche categories like GameDay, Mexico, Rainy Day, Pandora Local and Driving.

• Browse and choose one of the stations listed below **My Stations**, a list that will populate once you start adding stations or will be displayed immediately if you link to an existing account. Toggle Sort by date (date added) and Sort by A-Z to view the My Stations list. The first entry will always be Shuffle to mix the list randomly. There is a scroll bar on the side of the list of My Stations, but as I've said, it is difficult to see, being black on dark gray.

As usual, the Player will appear and at the bottom of the page and on the *Now Playing* page and can be used to control the music. Voice and Echo Spot screen controls work too.

CJ's Tips: I like Pandora, they have some great stations and I have no problem asking Alexa for a station based around an artist like, "Alexa, play Adele on Pandora," but things get more problematic when I ask for a themed playlist like "Alexa, play Laid Back Brunch on Pandora." There were many stations like this that got no response from Alexa even when I set Pandora as my default station service.

If you encounter this problem then the solution is simply to go to *Music, Video & Books > Pandora > Browse Genre* on the Alexa App and start a playlist playing. It will immediately be added as one of your stations and will appear under My Stations. *Now* try again to ask for it with your voice and you should have no problem.

iHeartRadio

This radio network and internet radio platform offers an immense amount of content including music and podcasts provided by 800 iHeartRadio partner stations in the US, more than 1,000 artist stations and a range of other media.

There are three membership levels:

- **iHeartRadio:** No cost, but you're limited to choosing a local radio station or curated stations built around well-known artists but including similar artists.

- **iHeartRadio Plus:** $4.99/month through Alexa; Play any song on demand; Unlimited skips; Save songs to create a single playlist; Replay songs from live radio and custom stations.

- **iHeartRadio All Access:** $9.99 through Alexa; Everything offered in Plus; Unlimited access to millions of songs; Listen offline on iOS and Android versions, but not yet on Alexa; Create as many playlists as you like.

I tried All Access but settled on the free iHeartRadio account simply because I've got so many other music choices that I don't need a paid service. If you start out with a free account, select the Upgrade Now tab on iHeartRadio at any time to try one of the paid plans.

Linking Alexa to iHeartRadio: Select **iHeartRadio** from the *Music, Video & Books* page and then *Link Your Account*. Authorize the link to an existing account or create a free or upgraded account with personal and payment information.

Using iHeartRadio on Echo Spot: The homepage has a search box where you can type in keywords including an artist's name, genre or city, for example. Searches return results related to your keyword, and they're divided into four categories:

- Stations — Artist Stations are titled after well-known artists to give you an idea of the flavor of the music, but each station includes songs from a range of artists. I'm currently listening to the station called Adele. The song Queue includes Rihanna, Ed Sheeran, Lorde, Ellie Goulding, OneRepublic and others in addition to Adele.

- Songs — Singles by title or group name related to the keyword.

- Artists — Bands, solo acts, choirs, etc. with names related to the keyword.

- Talk Shows — Shows and podcasts with names related to the keyword.

Your second option to locate music is the Browse section with three categories to look through:

- **Live Radio:** 800+ radio stations from around the country.

- **Shows:** These are mostly podcasts and the 20+ categories include Business & Finance, Comedy, Crime, Entertainment, Politics, Spirituality and Sports. Categories contain a dozen to more than 100 show options.

- **Favorites:** You have the option to select any station or show as a Favorite, and it will be saved here for easy locating later, though it might not show up immediately.

Manually select any Station and it will begin to play. You can also try using voice, but be as specific as possible for the most accurate results.

Once playing, the content can be controlled on the ***Now Playing*** page or with your voice. Also on the ***Now Playing*** page, you have the option to expand any selection in the **Queue** to:

- Tune the Station by choosing what you want to play — Top Hits, Mix or Variety. I don't know what the difference is between Mix and Variety, though perhaps seasoned iHeart enthusiasts will.

- Select the Station as a Favorite (check out my Tip below).

- Rate the song with thumb up or down symbols.

- Create a new station around your favorite artists.

- Shop Digital Music Store on Amazon for material from the artist — a new window will open to Amazon.

CJ's Tips: Again, you need to be very exact when asking Alexa for something from iHeartRadio, especially when asking for a radio station. I find saying "Alexa, play 102.7 KIIS-FM Los Angeles" is a bit of a mouthful and can be hard to remember precisely. I prefer to save my radio stations as favorites via the ***Now Playing*** page (as outlined above) and then I find that Alexa is much more likely to understand what I am requesting.

Tunein

Tunein is one of the oldest streaming services, founded in 2002. Today, its specialties are Music, News, Sports and Talk, and Tunein carries local, national and international content. Free and Premium accounts are available:

- Tunein: Free; Stream 600+ radio stations covering the range of styles
- Tunein Premium: $9.99/month; Stream 600+ radio stations; 40,000 audio books; No ads

Linking Alexa to Tunein: On the *Music, Video & Books* page, select *Tunein > Link your account > Authorize the link*. You can create an account there by providing the standard information, choosing the membership level you prefer and providing payment information if you choose Premium.

Using Tunein on Echo Spot: The Tunein homepage is set up much like the iHeartRadio page with a search box and more specific means of searching.

- Using the **Search Box** returns uncategorized results, unless you type in the exact name of the show or station you want, and that's a disadvantage compared with iHeartRadio. You're given a very long list of results to scroll through, and so I rarely use the function. Obviously, the more specific your search can be, the better results you'll get. You might have to try several searches using differing words or groups of words to find what you're looking for.
- The **Browse** function is more successful, and here Tunein has the edge on iHeartRadio. Select from:
  - Favorites, which is empty at first but will be populated as you "Favorite" content you like.

— Local Radio based on where you've given as your location at *Settings > Your Echo Spot > Device Location > Edit*

— Trending list of stations and shows currently popular.

— Music that is divided into 40+ subcategories for decade and musical genre.

— Talk with 30+ genre subcategories.

— Sports with 20+ subcategories including popular US, European and world sports, fantasy football and podcasts.

— News with a short list of trending shows from popular sources such as NPR, CNN and BBC, and two expandable subcategories: More Shows and Recent Episodes.

— By Location allows you to find news from continents and regions around the globe.

— By Language, with more than 90 languages offered.

— Podcasts broken into Music, Sports and Talk categories with a range of subcategories in each.

Once you choose a category > subcategory from Search or Browse results, a list of shows will be displayed for you to select from. Using the App for this purpose, rather than voice, is the best method.

CJ's Tips: Even if you know what you want, Alexa might have difficulty with your request if you use voice. For example, I said, "Play ESPN Outside the Lines," a popular show. Alexa replied, "Do you want me to add an outside station to your Pandora account?" No, but thanks for asking. The request, "Outside the Lines, ESPN" had Alexa take me to a random ESPN station. This again demonstrates that the more content available through Alexa, the more specific you'll need to be if using voice, and your request still might not produce the desired results. I use the App, and when I locate a station, show or podcast I want to return to, I "Favorite" it immediately, so I don't have to go searching for it later. Here's how:

• Go to the *Now Playing* page of the App

- If the show is at the top of the **Queue**, expand the options box using the down caret, select *Favorite Station,* and the words should light red while the Station is saved in your Favorites on the Tunein homepage, though it might not show there immediately

- If the show is in your History, then you'll have to select the show to play it and bring it to the top of the **Queue** where you can expand the box and select *Favorite Station*

SiriusXM

SiriusXM started by offering satellite radio services and has expanded into online radio where it's a good fit for Alexa and the Echo Spot. There are 70+ music channels, 20+ talk and entertainment channels, 10+ sports channels, 15+ news and issues channels, traffic and weather, Latin, Comedy and more.

Alexa's relationship with SiriusXM is different than it is with iHeartRadio, Tunein, Spotify and Pandora. SiriusXM is an Alexa Skill, so the platform isn't supported to the same extent as the other services. We'll cover Alexa Skills in detail in a later chapter. It being a Skill might be why the Alexa & SiriusXM connection is more problematic. I suggest you read the information on the SiriusXM page on the Alexa App for an overview and for ratings from users.

The service currently has 3/5 Stars or 60% favorable after about 1,000 ratings. Problems include connecting with and accessing SiriusXM, Alexa not recognizing login information or saying it is wrong, and linking to SiriusXM causing user's Echo devices to stop working entirely. The last issue is especially concerning, though I haven't experienced it. My experience has been that Customer Service at Sirius isn't up to speed about linking Amazon Alexa with SiriusXM at this writing.

Here's something else that might deter you from opening a new SiriusXM account, and it is due to it being a Skill rather than a fully supported service: you can't search or browse SiriusXM from the Alexa App. Using voice is the only current option. You must know the name of what you want to hear or use trial and error to find what you want.

I said, "Play football on SiriusXM." The first response was, "What do you want to hear?" When I asked again, the reply was, "I couldn't find a station called 'football' on SiriusXM."

If you want to proceed and have a SiriusXM account:

- Scroll to **SiriusXM** on the *Music, Video & Books* page.

- Select *Enable* and follow the prompts. If you do not have an account and still think it's worth checking out after the caveats given, sign up for an All Access trial or paid account at www. siriusxm.com/amazonalexa

- Sirius will send you a confirmation email.

- Select the link included to set up your password for your SiriusXM account and return to login to begin.

- Then, come back to the Alexa App to select *Enable* and make the connection.

CJ's Tips: Make sure popups are enabled in your browser or system settings. You might have to restart your computer after enabling popups to apply the change. The SiriusXM Skill can also be Enabled on Amazon's site here: www.amzn.to/2xa89GH

6: Tell Me a Story — Books

For any voice command you read in this chapter be sure to use your wake word ("Alexa", "Amazon", etc) first.

I must admit that I was not really that keen on the idea audiobooks (though I do love reading), but actually trying out the option on my Echo Spot whilst relaxing before bed has been something of a revelation, and one that I am enjoying exploring more and more. Here's how you too can listen to a vast library of written material using your Echo Spot:

Audible

Audible is an Amazon company, and its offerings have been significantly expanded in the last few years from just audiobooks to podcasts and original content that sounds more like a radio drama than a book because it is written for voice and read by a cast. For example, the X-Files: Cold Cases audiobook is four hours of material adapted from the series and read by David Duchovny, Gillian Anderson and other original and new actors. Audible books are read in the original reader's voice, not Alexa's.

Overview: An Audible account includes:

*   30-day Free Audible trial with one free book to keep.

* $14.95/month after with the option to cancel at any time.

*   1 book per month, and all books chosen during your subscription are yours to keep even if you cancel.

*   If you don't like a book, you have an exchange period for trading it for another.

*   Get 30% discount on additional books.

*   Free Audible app that allows you to listen on all your devices.

*   Listen/control on Echo Spot and other Echo devices with the Alexa App.

- Whispersync syncing that keeps your place in an audiobook even when you switch devices.

- 180,000 titles and growing daily.

- Limited free titles anytime.

Get Started: Here's how to get started with your Audible account

- Sign up for a free trial at www.audible.com

- Sign into your Amazon account.

- Choose Existing Payment Method (which will be indicated with its last 4 digits) or choose Add New Payment Method and complete its details.

- Select Start Your Membership.

- Select your free book.

- Cancel within 30 days to avoid being charged, if desired.

Connect: Once your Audible account is established, it's time to integrate Alexa/Echo Spot with Audible:

- Go to the Alexa App, choose **Music, Video & Books**.

- Select **Audible** from the Books section.

- Select **Link Account** and follow the prompts.

- If you already have an Audible account or have purchased Audible books in the past, the books will show up in the Audible section of the App ready to enjoy.

Listen: Here's how to enjoy your Audible audiobooks on your Echo Spot or mobile device:

- From the Audible section, select the title you want to hear using manual controls or voice.

- It will appear on Echo Spot and your Alexa App player.

- Use the available touch control options, if desired.

- Say, "Read my Audible book," and Alexa will ask which book, or you can request it by title.

- For books in progress, say, "Resume my Audible book".

- Use voice for controls like pause, go forward, go back, go to chapter 7, read louder and similar requests.

- You can also say things like, "Stop reading in 15 minutes" and "Set a 15 minute sleep timer" to have Alexa end reading when you want.

Kindle Books

Amazon's Kindle has been an innovate eBook reader since its introduction. Now you can listen to Kindle books with Alexa and Echo Spot — no Kindle needed. However, you should note that Kindle books are read in Alexa's voice.

Overview: You can purchase Kindle books individually or choose a Kindle Unlimited subscription. Here's what's offered:

- 30-day free Kindle Unlimited trial.

- Kindle Unlimited is $9.99/month and includes unlimited reading of 1 million book titles (new and recent books are not included) and magazines.

- Kindle books can also be borrowed, lent and rented. To find out more about these features visit www.amzn.to/2in5p6Q

- With an Amazon Prime membership, you can select one Kindle First early release book and borrow one additional book free each month.

Get Started: Here's how to create a Kindle account

- If you love audiobooks, consider a Kindle Unlimited 30-day trial, and the books can be read on a Kindle reader or Kindle for PC.

- To start a free trial, sign into your Amazon account from the Kindle Unlimited page (www.amzn.to/2vInb5Z)

- Choose Existing Payment Method (which will be indicated with its last 4 digits) or choose Add New Payment Method and complete its details.

- Select Start Your Membership.

- Cancel within 30 days to avoid being charged, if desired.

- If you don't want Kindle Unlimited, purchase, barrow, rent or select free Kindle books.

- If you already have a Kindle account, the books Alexa can read will show up in the Kindle section of the Alexa App.

Connect: Here's how to integrate Alexa/Echo Spot with Kindle:

- Go to the Alexa App, choose **Music, Video & Books**

- Select **Kindle Books** from the **Books** section

- You may be asked to select Link Account, and if so, follow the prompts given to establish the connection

- The Kindle books you select will appear in a list here

Listen: Here's how to enjoy your Kindle audiobooks on your Echo Spot:

- From the Kindle section, select the title you want to hear or use your voice to request it hands-free.

- The book will appear on Echo Spot and your Alexa App Player.

- Use the available touch control options, if desired, including selecting the chapter you want from the Player Queue.

- Use voice for controls like pause, go forward, go back, go to chapter 7, read louder and similar requests.

- You can also say things like, "Stop reading in 15 minutes" and "Set a 15 minute sleep timer" to have Alexa end reading when you want.

CJ's Tips: Selected books in the Audible and Kindle services can be listened to and read at the same time, something Amazon calls "immersion reading." Not only is the text in front of you on your phone or reader, but it is narrated and highlighted too. Amazon says this feature, "sparks an extra connection that boosts engagement, comprehension, and retention, taking you deeper into the book." Most people either love it or can't tolerate it, so if you want to give it a try, learn more at <u>www.audible.com/mt/Immersion</u>.

Now that we've gone through all your audio entertainment options you might want to return to Chapter 3 (page 27) about the ***Now Playing*** page to familiarize yourself with what that page of the Alexa App offers.

7: Write it Down & Get it Done — Lists

For any voice command you read in this chapter be sure to use your wake word ("Alexa", "Amazon", etc) first.

Alexa offers convenience you'll enjoy when making a Shopping List or To-do List. Both functions are explained in detail below.

To begin, choose the Lists tab from the Alexa App menu to see both **Shopping** and **To-do** headings. The default is to show the items on the Shopping List, but selecting the To-do List will display you its contents. Toggle back and forth to view and manage the lists.

Shopping Lists

Creating and managing a shopping list to take with you on your mobile app or to print is convenient, and you might find the process fun too, as I do. Here are your options:

Manually: Select *Shopping List* from the Lists page, type things you want to buy into the **Add Item** + box at the top of the page, and select the + sign or tap enter.

Voice: Say, "Add walnuts to the shopping list" regardless of the page showing on the Alexa App.

Manage your Shopping List: Whether inputted manually or by voice, the items will appear in the list with the most recent item at the top:

• Say, "Show my shopping list," and it will appear on the screen. Then say, "Remove brown rice from my shopping list" or "Remove item number 7 from my shopping list" to take it off the list. Saying "Check off" instead of "Remove" works too. Alternately, while the list is displayed on the Spot screen, swipe any item left to remove it.

- Check off a purchased or unwanted item by selecting the box to its left, and a ✔ will appear in the box, the item will be ~~crossed out~~, and the Delete option will appear on the right.

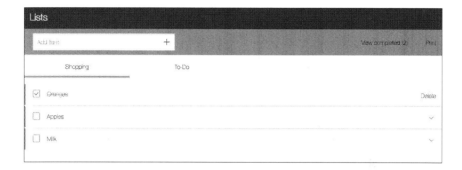

- Select the Delete option at right, if you want to remove it from the list, or leave it there as a reminder you've bought the item.

- Once you go away from the list and return, checked items you haven't deleted will be moved to the *Completed* list where they can be viewed or deleted individually or all at once.

- To print items, select the *Shopping* heading and *Print* from the header.

- Select the V-shaped down caret to the right for unchecked items on the Active list to:

  — Search Amazon for the item

  — Search Bing for the item

  — Move item to the To-do List

  — Delete item

Hear your Shopping List: I say, "Shopping list" to hear it because efficiency appeals to me. If you're more conversational, say "What's on my shopping list," or anything similar. The Alexa voice recognition technology has its voice-recognition "ears" open for "shopping list" almost regardless of what else you say. Try it!

View your Active and Completed Shopping List on the App:
Once you create a list, leave the page and return, there are two views of it available on the App. When on your Shopping List, toggle between Active and Completed at the top of the box. The Active list is items you haven't purchased or checked off. The Completed list is items you've checked off but haven't deleted.

View your Shopping List on Echo Spot: Any time you use voice to manage your list, the Shopping List will appear on the Echo Spot screen for about 30 seconds.

To-do Lists

There are just a few differences when creating and managing this list compared to the Shopping List.

Manually: Select *To-do* from the **Lists** page, and type tasks into the **Add Item** + box at the top of the page

Voice: Say, "Add call the accountant to the to-do list" regardless of the page showing on the Alexa App

Manage your To-do List: Regardless of how inputted, the items will appear in the list with the most recent item at the top

- Say, "Show my to-do list," and it will appear on the screen. Then say, "Remove repair the faucet from my to-do list" or "Remove item number 5 from my to-do list." Saying "Check off" instead of "Remove" works too.

- Check off a completed task by selecting the box to its left, and a ✔ will appear in the box, the item will be ~~crossed out~~, and the Delete option will appear on the right.

- Click or tap the *Delete* option at right if you want to remove it from the list, or leave it there as a reminder it is complete.

- Once you go away from the list and return, checked items you haven't deleted will be moved to the Completed list where they can be viewed or deleted individually or all at once.

- To print items, select the **To-do** heading and **Print** from the header

- Select the down caret to the right of items on the To-do list to:
  - Move item to the Shopping List
  - Delete item
  - See what Alexa heard, so you can adjust what you say (there doesn't seem to be any voice training related to this response)

Hear your To-do List: Unfortunately, saying, "To-do list" won't deliver a reading of the list. Instead, Alexa will ask, "What can I add to your To-do list," or similar. You will have to say, "Read my," "Tell me my," or "What is on my" To-do list.

View your To-do List on Echo Spot: The list is always visible on the App. To see it on the device, say "Show my To-do list" or similar.

View your Active and Completed To-do List Tasks on the App: Toggle between Active and Completed lists at the top of the box. The Active list is tasks you haven't finished. The Completed list includes tasks and projects you've checked off but haven't deleted.

CJ's Tips: When it comes to shopping lists I would say that the major failing is the inability to add more than one item at a time to your list by voice. For example, my Echo Show is perfectly placed in the kitchen and what I want to do is wander around and say "Alexa, add milk, bread, apples, ham and chicken to my shopping list" but that doesn't work. So it's great when I'm in the kitchen and remember one item I need to add but if I want to make a long list I'm better off adding it manually via the Alexa App.

As is the case when learning about any Echo device and Alexa talent, some casual practice with creating and managing Shopping and To-do Lists should prove fun and entertaining when a dose of patience is included!

Tweet your Accomplishments

Alexa supports a feature known as IFTTT or If This, Then That. One of the IFTTT tricks you can do is to have your Twitter account send a tweet that you've completed a task on your To-do list. I guess some accomplishments are worth letting the world know about! Go to www. ifttt.com/amazonalexa for this hack and many more.

8: Never Forget, Always Be On Time (& More) — Reminders, Alarms & Timers

For any voice command you read in this chapter be sure to use your wake word ("Alexa", "Amazon", etc) first.

For me, Alexa and the Echo Spot shine as a personal assistant in these categories. While reminders and alarms are similar, let's look at them separately to learn the nuances of each.

Reminders

This is a quick, easy way to avoid forgetting something urgent or important. A friend of mine stops by to see her elderly father several times a week and sets Reminders for him for the following day or two. When she can't get there in person, she calls her dad and does it remotely with her father's phone on Speaker mode.

Reminders can be set and managed manually or with voice, though using voice is easier.

To set and manage Reminders manually:

- Go to the *Reminders & Alarms* page where tabs for **Reminders, Alarms and Timers** appear.

- Select *Reminders*.

- Select + *Add Reminder*, and a form will appear.

- Fill in the spaces for Remind me to..., Date and Time.

- Select which device you want the reminder to be given on.

- Select *Cancel* or *Save* as appropriate.

- Your reminders appear on the Reminder page in chronological order of when they will occur, not when created.

- Manage any Reminder by selecting it, and you'll be taken to a page where you can Edit it or Mark as Completed.

- If you select *Edit*, you'll be taken to a page where you can edit the Reminder by selecting any of the details or *Delete* the Reminder.

- When editing a Reminder using the Alexa app on a computer, you must click away from the detail you edited, so that it is not highlighted, before the Save option becomes active.

To set and manage Reminders with voice:

- Say "Remind me to call the mechanic at 1pm"

- If you forget to give a time, Alexa will ask for one, and if you say "1," Alexa will ask, "Is that 1:00 in the morning or afternoon?" or similar.

- If you specify time but not date, Alexa will set up the reminder for today, so be sure to give the day, such as "tomorrow" or "Wednesday" for days this week, or give a date such as October 6.

- To cancel a Reminder, use the day and time rather than what you wanted to be reminded of, so say, "Cancel the reminder for 1pm today," and Alexa will ask for clarification if needed.

- **Note:** You cannot currently edit a Reminder using voice.

To see and manage Reminders on the Spot screen:

- Say, "Show my reminders" and the list will display.

- To cancel a Reminder, swipe it to the left, and it will disappear from the screen and the list in the App.

Completed Reminders: Select the Completed Reminders tab from below the active list to view them. You're not currently able to delete them from this list. They might jog your memory about whether you did something on the list, though being reminded of it is not a guarantee you followed through. For example, a completed reminder on this list doesn't mean a person remembered to take their medication or feed the dog!

Alarms

Alexa gives you a range of alarm options which we'll get to shortly, but first, here are the basics.

Setting and managing Alarms using voice:

- Say, "Set an alarm for 6am"

- Alexa will display the alarm and say, "Alarm set for 6am"

- Say "Cancel the alarm for 6am," and Alexa will say, "6am alarm canceled"

- If an alarm is on and you request another alarm for 7am, Alexa will say, "Second alarm set for 7am," and both alarms will show on the App

- For repeating alarms, say, "Set an alarm for":

  — 6am every day

  — 2pm every Friday

  — 7:30am on weekends

- If you forget to specify AM or PM, Alexa will ask, "Is that 6 in the morning or the evening?" and you can reply without using the wake word as long as the light circle on the Spot screen is green-blue to indicate Alexa is still listening

- If you don't respond, Alexa will ask again after a few seconds, and if you don't respond to the second query, no alarm will be set.

- All Alarms appear on the main Alarms page with boxes turned On/Off, indicators shown such as "Every day," with On alarms listed first.

Managing Alarms manually:

- Go to **Reminders & Alarms** and select **Alarms.**

- Use the box next to any alarm to turn it On and Off as desired.

- Select any Alarm to edit it, and a page will display where you can edit the Time, Alarm Sound, choose Repeats options including Never and Delete the alarm if you wish.

- When you've edited the alarm, select **Save Changes** or **Cancel**.

Manage Alarm Volume & Sound manually:

- Select **Manage alarm volume and default sound** from the main Alarms page, and you'll be taken to a page in Settings (though here, we discuss just sounds related to Alarms).

- Change the Alarm, Timer and Notification Volume by dragging the button on the slide bar (Note that this does not change the volume for any other device function, only the volume of the alarm itself).

- Under Custom Sounds, the **Alarm** box will show the Alarm Default Sound, which can be changed by expanding the box using the > shaped caret.

- From the list of **Alarm Default Sounds**, select Celebrity to see an expanded list of celebrities who have lent their voice to Alexa or scroll down Custom sounds to select one.

CJ's Tips: If you set up an alarm to go off at the same time every day of the week you won't be able to cancel that alarm for just one day if you don't need it, you have to cancel the whole weekly alarm. Consequently, although it takes me a little longer to set up, I tend to set up an alarm for each day that I need it giving me full control over each alarm.

Also, do check out Celebrity alarm sounds, these change over time and some of them are pretty funny. Failing that, the more traditional alarm sounds are worth exploring to find the one that suits you best.

Timers

If you're like me, you may well use Timers for a range of purposes, some which overlap with Reminders. These are simple functions, so this can be quick:

- Timers can be set for 1 second to 24 hours.

- Timers must be set with voice, so say, "Set a timer for 45 minutes" or "Cancel the timer".

- You can name a timer so try saying, "Set pizza timer for 10 mins"

- Multiple timers can be set to run concurrently.

- Active timers will display on the screen for a few seconds at the beginning or if you say, "Show me the timer".

- Active timers will display and count down on the App.

- Timers are also cancelled by swiping them left when they're displayed on the device screen or by selecting them on the App and choosing Cancel.

- Select Manage timer volume to be taken to the Settings page to adjust Alarm, Timer and Notification Volume.

CJ's Tips: Multiple named timers are so great in the kitchen when you're cooking. Set and name timers for every element of the meal you're making so each timer also becomes a reminder of what's finished cooking or what needs to happen next.

9: Keep it Simple — Routines

For any voice command you read in this chapter be sure to use your wake word ("Alexa", "Amazon", etc) first.

Routines is a new feature, but one I've been waiting on for quite some time. The number of things that I can do with Alexa and my Echo devices has grown rapidly over that last 12 months. This also means that the amount of time I spend "talking" to Alexa has grown too. To date, every time I want Alexa to do something I have to give her a voice command for *each* thing and sometimes that can be a drag. I previously mentioned in the Lists chapter that if I want to add items to my shopping list by voice then I have to do it one item at a time... "Alexa add oranges to my list," "Alexa, add apples to my list," "Alexa, add bananas to my list" etc, etc. If I have 20 items to add to my shopping list at once this can get really old, really quickly.

Well, although the **Routines** feature doesn't yet solve that little conundrum it is a step in the right direction and shows me that Amazon is now addressing the question of how to activate several functions at once with just one voice command.

So here's the idea of Routines. We all have daily habits and routines, from getting up and dressed in the morning to coming home from work and cooking dinner in the evening. Now you can group certain Alexa features together to compliment those daily routines and have them all start/activate at the same time, either with one single voice command or at a set time each day.

For example, if you wake up at the same time each day you can program a morning routine for Alexa to turn up your thermostat, turn on your Smart Home kettle, give you the weather forecast and catch you up on news headlines via your Flash briefing. Either set this routine to start at 6.30 am every morning or start the routine by saying something like

"Alexa, start the day" or "Alexa, good morning" or whatever you like!

So that's the good news about Routines. The slightly less good news is that, at the time of writing, the actions that you can program as part of a routine are limited to Smart Home devices, your News briefing, your Traffic information and a weather forecast. Personally, while I do use Alexa's news, traffic and weather features, they are not so important to me that I need to schedule them for a set time each day. Bunching the operation of several Smart Home devices into one request is certainly welcome but I already have the ability to do that via Smart Home Groups (discussed later in this guide).

So Routines is a great idea and one that I think will become very useful in the future as more options are added. What I would really like is the ability to set up a morning routine where Alexa reads me my calendar appointments for the day and then starts playing my favorite radio station or music playlist. I suspect options like these will become available soon.

For now, let's look at how to setup a routine. Go into your Alexa App on a mobile device and tap the **Menu icon** (top left) and then **Routines**. You will see that Alexa has already set up a basic routine entitled "Alexa, Start my day". For now, ignore this and tap the **+ sign** at the top right of the page.

Now you will have the options to **Add cue** and **Add action**. Tap the + *sign* next to **Add cue** and either create a voice command for your routine (eg, "Alexa, good morning") or schedule a set time for your routine. When scheduling a time, you not only set the time of day but can choose to have the routine happen on a specific day, every day, week days or weekends. When you've chosen your schedule or voice command tap *Done*.

Now tap the + *sign* next to **Add action**. You will now be able to choose from the 4 options I mentioned earlier, *News, Smart Home, Traffic* and *Weather*. Setting up all these features are discussed in the following chapters of this guide. For now, all you need to know is that you can tap *Add* to include one or all of these features to your new Routine and then tap *Create*.

Your new routine will now appear in your list of routines and you can tap again on any routine to edit it, temporarily toggle the routine on or off, and delete the routine if you wish. I suggest you read on now and return to this chapter when you have read the Smart Home chapter (page 80) and the Things to Try chapter (page 87) where I discuss linking Smart Home devices to Alexa and setting up news, traffic and weather briefings.

CJ's Tips: In the upcoming Smart Home chapter I discuss how to put several Smart Home devices into Groups for convenience. One thing that Routines can do, that Smart Home Groups can't, is to activate a number of devices at a set time of the day (or night). This is an aspect of Routines that is already very useful for me. I like certain lights in my home to come on and switch off at certain times of the day, especially when I am away from home and want to give the impression that the house is still occupied. Scheduling these lighting states for set times and set days is now a breeze with Alexa Routines.

10: Let's See What She Can Do — Alexa Skills

For any voice command you read in this chapter be sure to use your wake word ("Alexa", "Amazon", etc) first.

Alexa Skills are like "apps" for your Echo device. In the same way that you download apps to your tablet or phone for added functionality, you can add (enable) Skills for Alexa that allow you to do more and get more out of your Echo device. Adding and using these skills is super easy and there are currently more than 15,000 Skills to choose from, and the number grows daily. Skills are loosely grouped into 20 categories currently. Some are good, many are bad, there are sure to be a few of interest for every Echo owner. For an overview of Alexa Skills visit: www.amzn.to/2z05vBM

Get Familiar with Skills: Start your Skills adventure by getting to know what's available. There are three ways to browse Skills, and all begin on the *Skills* page on the Alexa App menu. The default setting on this page is to show All Skills. Near the top right is a tab called Your Skills, which will be populated as you enable Skills for your use. Once you are adding Skills, you'll likely toggle back and forth between the All Skills and Your Skills lists quite a bit. OK, let's explore starting on the *Skills* page in the Alexa App.

Option 1: Scan the rows of Skills labeled Top, Recommended, Trending, New, Most entertaining, etc. Each row can be scrolled horizontally using the arrow at the right to view additional Skills in the category.

Option 2: Explore the **Categories tab** which jumps you down the page to where Skills are organized in 20 categories including:

- Newest Arrivals

- Business & Finance

- Food & Drink

- Games, Trivia & Accessories

- Health & Fitness

- Movies & TV

- Music & Audio

- News

- Productivity

- Shopping

Select any category to browse the Skills in it. On each category page there will be two rows of Skills that can be browsed by sliding left or using the arrow on the right of the page, these are:

- **Recommended for You** based on Skills you already have, your search history and other factors Amazon plugs into an algorithm to determine what you might like.

- **Top Enabled Skills** based on the popularity of the Skills.

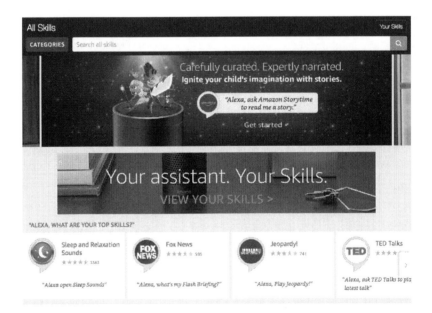

CJ's Tips: These rows are followed by a list of all the Skills in the category. It can be a long list! Currently, there are nearly 500 Skills in the Health & Fitness category, so rather than scrolling through the options, I used the search box to narrow the list to skills related to a personal interest such as biking. Four results appeared. If there were many results, I would use the Sort By option at the top right of the results list to narrow the search by Relevance (default), Average Rating or Release Date.

Option 3: Use the Search box to find a Skill for something very specific (e.g., ecobee, weather Canada, Corvette) or to see if there is one related to one of your interests. For a random sampling, I typed in:

- "Chinese" and received 35 search results related to learning the language or one of the dialects, cuisine, the Chinese calendar and zodiac, etc.

- "Flowers" — 17 results about ordering flowers, facts and trivia, state flowers, etc.

- "Michigan" — 89 results about trivia, history, several state universities, winning lottery numbers, snow reports for skiing, information from news outlets, etc.

Again, the results can be narrowed using the Sort By options at the top right of the results list or by adding a word or two to your search query — "Chinese language", or "University of Michigan", for example. For something like "news" with more than 3,200 results, you'll have to search a specific news organization, news about a topic, city, event or similarly narrow term.

Enable Alexa Skills and Use Them

Skills are super easy to set up and use. There's no downloading required and most can be activated just with your voice if you know what you're looking for. When you're ready to put a Skill into action, the first step is to enable it, which is like turning it on for use with your Alexa account and Echo devices.

Here's how to enable and use an Alexa Skill:

- Use one of the options above to locate a skill you want to enable, and select the skill. A full page description for that particular skill will appear.

- Select **Enable Skill**, and after a few seconds, the box will switch to **Disable Skill**, which means it's been enabled and will appear in the Your Skills list.

- Alternately, say, "Alexa, enable the Rainforest Sounds Skill" (for example).

- You can also browse and Enable Skills on Amazon.com here: www. amzn.to/2iGfA6u

- To use any Enabled Skill, include the name of the Skill when making a request such as "Alexa, play rainforest sounds".

- **Note:** Skills in use do not appear on the **Now Playing** page or Player, so to control them, say "Stop," "Pause," "Resume" or similar.

Disable an Alexa Skill

Over time, the Your Skills section can become crowded with Skills you don't use. They're easy to remove.

- Select the Skill from Your Skills list.

- Select Disable Skill, and the box will flip to Enable Skill to indicate it isn't enabled and the Skill will disappear from your list.

CJ's Tips: It's important to note that some of the Skills require creating and/ or linking to an account or subscription separate from Amazon, so additional steps might be required. This is just as straightforward as the account linking that you would have done for some of the music services described in Chapter 5. For example, if you want to order an Uber cab or a Domino's pizza then you will need to link Alexa to the accounts you hold with those companies. Clicking the **Enable** button will automatically open a window for you to sign in to your account or set one up if you don't yet have one.

While you're on the full description page for a Skill, and before you enable it, take a moment to familiarize yourself with what it offers, how it works and what others think about it. It's very tempting, when you first start browsing Skills, to go a bit crazy and start enabling dozens of new skills straight away... I don't recommend it... you just end up with lots of Skills that you either don't like, don't know how to use or forget that you even have!

I always read the following...

1. **About this skill:** You might be surprised how often your expectation of what a Skill will do is very different from what it actually does.

2. **Try Saying:** Pay attention to these commands as they are probably the only ones that work, so you'll need to remember them.

3. **Invocation Name:** Found under "Skill Details", you will certainly need to remember the invocation name of the Skill as this is the name that Alexa is listening for to identify the Skill you're trying to use.

4. **Reviews:** It's definitely worth checking out the best and worst reviews of a Skill. I like to see at least a dozen reviews for any given Skill and a star rating of 4 stars and above. I will look at skills with lower star ratings if I think the Skill is going to be really useful. The Domino's Pizza Skill is a good example. It has a lot of negative one star reviews from users who couldn't make the Skill work or had a bad experience. I liked the idea of easy voice ordering so gave it a try for myself and it works fine for me... mainly because I always order the same pizza... every time!

Develop an Alexa Skill and Share It with the World

As you browse Skills, you'll notice the name of the developer next to each. There are Skills from large companies like Capital One and Starbucks, but most of the 15,000+ Skills are developed by small companies, entrepreneurs and hobbyists.

Amazon has a Developers Site dedicated to creating Skills where you can go through the process: Learn/Design/Build/Launch. The Amazon Skills Kit (ASK) is an online center for developers. Build one from scratch or use templates available for several types of skills. Amazon offers rewards to developers such as Echo devices, Amazon dev shirts and Amazon Web Services (AWS) credits.

CJ's Tips: I've explored more than 500 Skills and Enabled more than 200 in the last few months. My Skills list currently has 44 Skills; I use some daily and others only occasionally.

The Skills I rely on the most are those that save me time, are easy to use and/or offer genuine value. If they're a hassle, a time-waster or not the easiest or best way to do things, I either disable them immediately or as soon as the novelty wears off. Some have features that are easy to use while some have features that are a hassle. Alexa Skills are still very new and there are quite a few bugs in some that need to be ironed out. My experience is that the simple Skills work best while the more ambitious Skills fall short. For example quiz Skills and ambient sound Skills deliver what they promise, whereas recipe Skills often come up short, because the technical requirements of searching through an enormous database of recipes and delivering step by step instructions via Alexa appear to be out of reach for the time being.

You'll also notices that there are sometimes several Skills that do the same thing. Searching Skills for "find my phone" yielded six results, "restaurant finder" showed ten options and "control lights" produced a list of 25 smart home Skills.

When I'm undecided about which of two or three Skills to choose, I enable both or all and use them alternately. I often use one right after another, and do that every day for a week or so. This is a better way to determine which Skill is right for me than to try one for a week and then try another. I like an immediate, one-after-the-other comparison.

The point I'm delicately trying to make is that there are many Skills that... just aren't very good. It's worth putting in some time to find the gems that you'll use over and over, but be prepared to wade through quite a lot of rubbish!

11: 21st Century Living — Smart Home

For any voice command you read in this chapter be sure to use your wake word ("Alexa", "Amazon", etc) first.

If you're already integrating smart technology into your home, then learning to control it with Alexa's help will be one of the easier parts of the curve. There's a four-step process that is straightforward and usually successful. If you're new to smart home devices then I recommend you visit the Amazon Smart Home page (www.amzn.to/2wHRFJW) to familiarize yourself with the possible options.

Smart home tasks are considered Skills and used as such. You'll be well-prepared for the information here if you've read the previous chapter and enabled a few Skills.

Here are the steps. Each is explained in detail below:

1. Prepare your smart home device for linking.

2. Enable the Skill associated with the smart home device.

3. Ask Alexa to discover the device to connect the two and to use Alexa to control the smart home device.

4. Use the Alexa App to organize your smart home devices for optimal use.

Amazon suggests we cover a few common-sense security tips for using smart home devices with Alexa, so let's do that first:

• Follow the device's instructions for safe, recommended uses.

• Confirm that requests have been carried out — especially tasks related to your home's safety and security (security system, exterior lighting, door locks, garage door, HVAC, appliances, and similar).

- Turn off the microphones on Echo Spot and other Alexa devices if you do not want Alexa to respond to voice commands when safety and security cannot be ensured (such as when adults are away from home).

- Remember that once a device is connected, anyone can use Alexa/ Echo Spot to control it, so make sure those in your household and guests understand safe operation of smart home devices.

Okay, let's get rolling.

Step 1: Prepare your Smart Home Device

This step ensures your device is compatible and optimized for use with Alexa:

- Verify that your smart home device is compatible with Amazon Alexa, which can be done by searching for it on the Skills page of the Alexa App or Amazon.com, checking the packaging, contacting the manufacturer or viewing its website and looking for the device on the Alexa smart home shopping page (amzn.to/2wITbeJ) that includes all compatible devices.

- Download the manufacturer's app for the smart home device to any mobile device (preferably the same one that you're using to manage the Alexa App).

- Use the manufacturer's app to set up the smart home device/ equipment on the same Wi-Fi network your Echo Spot is on.

- Download and install the latest software updates for the smart home device.

Step 2: Enable the Device's Skill

If your smart home device is compatible with Alexa, it will have its own Skill.

- Locate the Skill by going to the main *Skills* page on the Alexa app, clicking *Categories* then *Smart Home* and using the search box to find the relevant Skill. Alternately, Skills can be searched on Amazon.com (www.amzn.to/2iGfA6u).

- Select the Skill.

- Read the **About** information and the **Skill Details** on the Skill page that opens to familiarize yourself with its capabilities.

- Select the *Enable* button, and when it changes to *Disable*, you'll know the Skill is enabled.

- When prompted, sign into the smart home device account to link it to your Alexa account.

- Follow any prompts given to complete setting up the smart home device on Alexa.

Note: A list of your Enabled smart home devices will populate on the *Smart Home* page in your Alexa App. Select any of the Skills to Disable it or to learn more about it.

Step 3: Ask Alexa to Discover the Device

This can be done two ways:

- Say, "Discover devices".

- Go to the *Smart Home* page on the App, select *Devices*, and then select the *Discover* tab.

Step 4: Set Up Groups and Scenes for Your Smart Home Devices

As you connect smart home devices to Alexa, you can then set them up to work together by putting them into groups or scenes.

It may seem at first that there is no real difference between the Group option and the Scenes option; but in fact they have different functions.

Basically, when your smart home devices are put together in a Group the command you can give them via Alexa is simply to turn those devices on or off simultaneously, so for example turning on three specific light bulbs in the bedroom at the same time.

However, the Scenes option allows you to predetermine the state of those devices, for example if you want the light bulbs to be on low and the thermostat to go down to a lower temperature at bedtime (in this case the Scene would be named Bedtime and the command to Alexa would be "Alexa, turn on Bedtime").

The other big difference is that you set up a Group within the Alexa App; whereas to set up Scenes you need to first configure those scenes in the smart home device's app, and then those specific device scenes will be listed in the **Scenes** page on the Alexa App, where you can then control those scenes via Alexa.

Effectively the **Scenes** page simply shows you the different scenes you have already set up and then allows you to manage them with Alexa voice commands.

How to Set Up Groups:

Chose the **Groups** tab on the main **Smart Home** page:

- Choose **Create Group** to connect two or more devices that will work together with a single command.

- Follow any additional prompts to complete formation of the Group including naming the group and selecting devices for the group.

- Try the Group by making a request of Alexa appropriate to the Group's functionality ("Turn on the lights," or "Lock the doors," for example).

- To edit the Group, select it and choose the name to change it or select/deselect devices you want in the group.

- To delete a group, select **Delete this group**.

CJ's Tips: Alexa uses voice recognition to understand what you say and connect it with digital content such as the name of a group you type into the App. For this reason, give groups names that won't confuse Alexa. To be on the safe side, I recommend sticking with the Common Group names that Alexa offers.

How to Manage Scenes:

First configure specific Scenes within the smart home device's app. For example, if you want to create a scene with the Philips Hue smart light, then you need to go into the Hue app to set up that scene.

Then choose the **Scenes** tab on the main **Smart Home** page:

- All Scenes that you have set up on your smart home devices should appear, meaning that you can use voice command to activate those Scenes, using the name you've set for that Scene ("turn on Bedtime" for example).

- If you don't want Alexa to control a certain Scene, then click on **Forget** to delete the Scenes from the Alexa App

If Alexa Doesn't Discover your Smart Home Device

Try these tips in this order. They will troubleshoot and solve most issues.

Device Issues:
- Double-check that:
  — Your smart home device is compatible with Alexa.
  — That you have Enabled the device's Skill.
  — That you have downloaded the device's app.
  — That you have downloaded the latest software updates for the device.

— For a Philips Hue Bridge, be sure to press the button on the Bridge before trying to discover devices.

Note: Additional details for these steps are found in the four steps above.

- Restart your Echo devices including Echo Spot, and restart your smart home device.

- Disable and Enable the smart home device.

- In the Alexa App, choose the Forget option for the smart home device to unlink it from Alexa, and then try to reconnect it.

Wi-Fi Issues: The Echo Spot and your smart home devices must be on the same Wi-Fi network. Personal networks are best; school and work networks you don't control might not allow unrecognized devices to connect.

Check or change the Wi-Fi network for Echo Spot by:

- Choosing Settings for the Echo Spot.

- Observing what network the Spot is on beneath the Wi-Fi option.

- Changing the Wi-Fi network your Echo Spot is on, if necessary.

- Using the Add a Network option to add a network for your Echo Spot and smart home devices.

Note: Some smart home devices can only connect to the 2.4 GHz Wi-Fi band. If you have a dual-band network, make sure it is set to the 2.4 GHz band.

Change confusing group names: Remember that Alexa won't comprehend words with numbers or symbols in them like kitch3n lights or #kitchen lights@, so make changes to group names, if necessary.

Discover your smart home devices again: If you've made any changes discussed here, including the Wi-Fi network or band or a group name say, "Discover devices." Alexa will let you know if they are found or will say "I didn't find any devices." If this occurs, contact the smart home device manufacturer for further assistance, since it is up to the device manufacturer, not Amazon, to ensure that their devices are compatible with Alexa devices.

12: Your Highly Capable Personal Assistant — Things to Try

For any voice command you read in this chapter be sure to use your wake word ("Alexa", "Amazon", etc) first.

This is a large section of the Alexa App and could be a book of its own. There is an abbreviated section of Things to Try on the Echo Spot screen at **Settings > Things to Try.**

The good news is that many of the Things to Try have been discussed in other sections, and the ones I don't talk about anywhere are very straightforward and easy to use with the few words of explanation given in the Alexa App. Our purpose in this chapter is to shed light on Things to Try that haven't been mentioned but require some explanation.

To get started, select the **Things to Try** from the menu in the Alexa App to explore them for yourself or to follow along with this discussion. The Things to Try section is just a list. When you select any of them, you will usually be taken to the Help & Feedback section for an explanation. The list serves as an easy place to find topics you want more information about. Things to Try is also accessible on the screen. Slide down to show options, and tap **Settings**. Slide the screen up to show **Things to Try**. The list is not in the same order on the screen and on the App.

Here are some of the useful and interesting Things to Try that haven't been detailed already in the book:

What's new?

I like to keep up with Alexa's capabilities, so I check this section weekly, at least. There's always something new. It's a mixed and disorganized bag ranging from simple, fun stuff ("Drum roll") to interesting information (the ability to give publication dates and authors for popular books) to new Skills ("Give me a quote") to new Alexa-enabled devices (this week, TV remotes from Sony, Logitech and Broadlink). It's a potpourri of fresh possibilities with Alexa and Echo Spot.

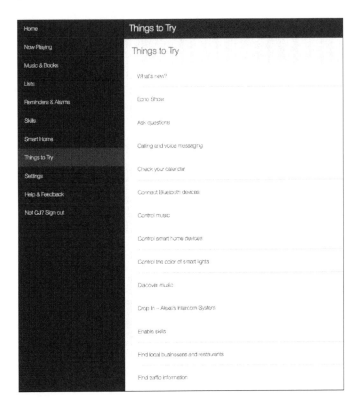

Ask Questions

If you can think it, the question might be worth asking. I ask these types of questions quite often:

- What time it is here or elsewhere?

- Conversions of weight, measurements temperature, money.

- Spellings/synonyms/definitions.

- People and place facts.

- Math.

Check and Manage Your Calendar

Alexa can link to calendars from Google, Apple and Microsoft.

- Go to **Settings**, and scroll down to the **Accounts** section to **Calendar**.

- Choose the calendar you want to connect, and select **Link _____ account.**

- Link another calendar, if desired.

- Say, "Show me my calendar," "What's on my calendar?" "What's my next appointment?" or similar.

- Say, "Add a 9:30am meeting to my calendar".

Discover new Alexa Skills

See Chapter 10 (page 73) dedicated to Alexa Skills, but if you want to hear about the latest releases:

- Say, "What are popular Skills?"

- Say, "What new Skills do you have?"

- Browse the Skills store (www.amzn.to/2xOQ9pi) mentioned earlier where every Skill can be found and Enabled.

Find Local Businesses and Restaurants & Reviews

If you haven't set your location yet, this is a good time to do that, so Alexa knows where to search. In the App **Settings**, select **your device**. In the **General** section of your device's settings, select **Device location** and **Edit**, if the location is incorrect. Add as little as your zip code or as much as your full address. The more information you provide, the more accurate Alexa can be in telling you how far you are from businesses and restaurants.

With Echo Spot, results will be displayed on the screen, with the business name, a short description, its distance from your location and Yelp rating with number of reviews. To see more results, slide the screen left. Use the touch screen to select a listing for its street address, phone number and business hours, if available. Here are things to try:

- "Find a Mexican restaurant".
- "Is the post office open?"
- "What clothing stores are nearby?"
- "What supermarkets are near me?"
- "What is the phone number for B&V Asian Market?"

Your search doesn't have to be local either. When planning a trip, you can ask Alex to find any of these things in another town.

- "Is there a shoe store in Grand Rapids?"
- "Pharmacy in Plano, Texas".
- "Is there Crossfit in Raleigh, North Carolina?"

All searches produce Cards, so you'll have the results right in front of you on the Alexa App, which is often a better place to view them compared to the small screen of the Spot. Search results might be varied, especially when there are only a few good options. When using Alexa in a rural area, I requested a "sporting goods store," and got one accurate result and four others, ranging from a used firearms dealer to a marina. See how you do with your searches!

CJ's Tips: Alexa is far from perfect yet, but I'm often impressed with the information I can get from her. If I need to call a local shop or business I always ask Alexa for the number first before reaching for the phone book or doing a search online; more often than not, I get the info I'm looking for.

Find Traffic Information

Alexa can give you an estimated time for your commute and the fastest route.

- In **Settings** on the Alexa App, scroll to the **Accounts** section.

- Select **Traffic.**

- Add or change your current address, your "From,".

- Add a destination, your "To".

- Stops along the way can be added too.

- Later, select **Change address** to edit any of the locations.

While I use this for the drive I make most often, it can be convenient for determining the time for other driving routes by changing the "From," "To" or both.

Weather Information

Once Alexa knows your location in **Settings** > **Your Device** > **Location**, you can hear or view local weather information on Echo Spot and on the Card produced. Ask about weather in other cities around the globe too. Common questions Alexa can answer include:

- "What's the weather?"

- "Show me the forecast".

- "Will it rain tomorrow?"

- "How warm will it be today?"

There are many ways to answer the question, but Alexa replies to all of them with the same information — verbally sharing current and expected weather conditions for the next 24 hours and showing an extended forecast within the App or on the screen.

Go to the Movies

This section uses your location to access local movie schedules and can give you information for movie schedules in cities you'll be visiting. I get the best results with questions like these:

- "What movies are playing?"

- "What movies are playing at [name of theater complex]?"

- "When will Indiana Jones play tomorrow?"

- "Show me the trailer for the movie Dunkirk".

- "Tell me about the Aquaman movie".

Hear the News

Alexa offers something called a Flash Briefing. Many news and entertainment organizations including NPR, NBC, FOX, BBC and ESPN make brief overviews of the news, such as you might hear at the top or bottom of the hour, and those summaries can be added to your Flash Briefing.

To select which summaries you want to hear in your Briefing, and to start and manage it:

- Go to **Settings > Flash Briefing** to toggle On or Off the default options, if there are any.

- Go to Skills and search your favorite news, sports, weather and entertainment stations (there are new media coming onboard every week), and enable the Skill.

- If it offers a Briefing summary, that will show in your list of Flash Briefing choices in Settings.

- Toggle On or Off the briefings, and you can make changes when desired.

- Ask "What's the news," "Give me my flash briefing," "Flash briefing," "What's in the news?" or something similar, and you'll hear the entire briefing, one organization at a time.

- If the news organization offers video with its briefing, it will play on the Echo Spot screen.

- The briefing does not show on the Now Playing page or the Player, but on the touch screen, your Flash Briefing can be controlled with standard control buttons.

CJ's Tips: Go to *Settings > Flash Briefing > Edit Order* in the Alexa App on a mobile device. Now you can tap and drag each of your news sources into your preferred order of importance. I find that there are a couple of news sources I value above the others, so I definitely want to hear them first.

Sports: Keep Up with Your Pro and College Sports Teams & More

Give Alexa a team name and say, "score," and you'll hear the score of the most recent game. If you want to hear the latest scores and the next game for all the teams you follow, go to *Settings > Sports* to search and select those teams. Then, you'll get the answer when you ask questions like:

- "Sports scores".
- "When do the Seattle Mariners play next?"
- "NBA scores".
- "Score for Real Madrid".
- "How many touchdowns did Odell Beckham junior score?"
- "How many homeruns does Aaron Judge have?"

Many major colleges can be followed too in football and basketball. The leagues currently supported on the Alexa App are:

North American Leagues:

- MLB — Major League Baseball
- MLS — Major League Soccer
- NBA — National Basketball Association
- NCAA — National Collegiate Athletic Association
- NFL — National Football League
- NHL — National Hockey League

- WNBA — Women's National Basketball Association

European Leagues:

- English Premier League

- FA Cup — Football Association Challenge Cup

- German Bundesliga

- UEFA Champions League

CJ's Tips: Above is a list of all the teams officially supported via Alexa, but I've found that I can get information for many other teams just by searching for them in the search box at **Settings > Sports Update** within the Alexa App.

Shop Amazon (for Prime Members)

Did you hear about the 6-year old girl in Texas who ordered a dollhouse with Alexa or Jimmy Kimmel's prank of telling Alexa to order pool noodles during his show broadcast into millions of US homes?

These are cautionary tales about shopping via Alexa, but with precautions, you'll be immune from such surprises.

To shop on Amazon, you'll need:

- A Prime membership (a 30-day free trial is available).

- A US shipping address.

- A payment method stored with Amazon in your account's 1-Click settings.

- Voice Purchasing enabled in the Alexa App at **Settings > Voice Purchasing**.

- (Optional) A 4-digit code in **Voice Purchasing** that you'll have to give as a safeguard against unauthorized shopping, accidental purchases and not-so-funny pranks.

- Use **Manage 1-Click Settings** in this section to be sure you have a payment method connected to 1-Click.

- An Echo device and the Alexa App.

Once you're set up, you can browse on Echo Spot and order Prime-eligible items with Alexa. Here's how my shopping with Alexa usually goes when I'm not sure which product I want:

- I say, "Shop coffee makers," and then browse them on the screen.
- I select Details of any product to learn more including color options, sizes or to **Add to Cart**.
- When I make the decision to buy, I select "Buy This," and the order is placed.
- If I get buyer's regret immediately, I say, "Cancel my order," and it's cancelled.
- Canceling orders after a short time must be done online.
- When the order ships, Alexa gives me a voice notification that also shows up in *Settings > Notifications.*

When I know what I want, the process is much shorter:

- "Order _____," and Alexa will ask you to confirm the order or will show several options on the Echo Spot screen.
- "Reorder _____," and Alexa will ask for confirmation.
- "Add _____ to my cart," is an option too, and you can then go online to review your cart and place the order.

You can also buy digital music with Alexa if you have a US billing address and payment method stored with Amazon that is issued by a US bank. Amazon.com gift cards can be used too.

Physical goods ordered can be tracked with a simple request, "Track my order."

Calling and Messaging

This feature has tremendous potential and will become more useful as the universe of Alexa users expands. If you know three or more people with Alexa Enabled devices, this section might be worth reading now. Otherwise, it's here when Alexa catches on more broadly among your friends, family members and business contacts. You can communicate with other Alexa users if you both have downloaded the Alexa App (note that, non-Echo users can also download the App onto their phone), set up this Skill and input the contact's information correctly:

Setting up Calling & Messaging

- Download the latest Alexa App for iOS 9.0 or higher here: www. apple.co/2xhWycQ

- Or for Android 5.0 or higher here: www.bit.ly/2fBWcUi

- Select the Conversations icon 🔘 on the App home page of your mobile phone, and follow the instructions to sign up for Calling & Messaging and to verify your mobile number.

- Import your contacts, and those who have signed up for Calling & Messaging will appear in your contact list.

- To add or edit contacts for this service, update your phone's local Address book and then open the Alexa App.

- Give your contacts names you'll remember, ask Alexa to call one of them, and Alexa will dial the number associated with that name.

- Calling & messaging can be used on Echo, Echo Spot, Echo Show and Echo Dot or between non-Echo users that have the Alexa App on their phone.

- If you ever wish to deregister from Calling & Messaging, contact Amazon customer service at 1.877.375.9365.

Using Calling & Messaging for Calls

- Tell your Alexa-using friends and family about Calling & Messaging, and encourage them to get set up and begin using the service whether they have Echo, Echo Spot, Echo Show or Echo Dot (though obviously only Echo Spot and Echo Show offer video calling).

- To make a call from Echo Spot, say, "Call Aunt Ellen," and Alexa will begin the call.

- If you prefer, say, "Turn video off," or select the Video icon on the touch screen.

- To make a call from the Alexa App, select the Conversations icon ▣ , select the New Conversation icon, select a contact and the Phone icon for an audio-only call or the camera icon for a video call.

- When someone is calling you, Alexa will let you know who is calling and display the contact on the screen, a green light will appear on your Echo device.

- To answer a call, say, "Answer".

- To ignore the call, say, "Ignore the call".

- To end a call, say, "Hang up" or tap the Echo Spot screen and select the end-call button.

- **There's a video about calling with Alexa here:** www.amzn. to/2vJrgXz

Using Calling & Messaging for Messages

- Messages are recorded and played back to the recipient rather than transcribed and read by Alexa.

- To send a message from Echo Spot, say, "Send a message to Sara Smith," and Alexa will prompt you for the message and send your message when you complete it.

- To send a message from the Alexa App, select the Conversations icon ▣ , select the New Conversation icon, and select a contact before following the prompts, or you can select the Keyboard icon and type a message before hitting the Send button.

- To reply to a message from the App, select the conversation from those shown, and press the Microphone icon while speaking your message, releasing it when done to send the message or sliding left to cancel the message.

- To hear messages on the Echo Spot, say, "Play my messages".

- When more than one phone number is synced with Alexa, you can name the numbers and say, "Play messages for _____" to hear only your messages.

- To review messages on the App, choose the Notifications icon or go to Conversations to view those with a New Notification icon, and then choose between hearing the messages and reading a transcription of them.

- **There's a video about messaging with Alexa here:** www.amzn.to/2wSzRfk

Drop in

- Drop in is typically set up among devices in a single household, between family members and BFFs.

- Drop in means that people in separate parts of the home or in different homes can communicate immediately without making a formal call, or it allows you to see what's going on in the kids' room when connected to another Echo Spots or an Echo Show in that room.

- Drop in must be enabled in the mobile Alexa App for all devices that will use the capability.

- In the Conversations section of the mobile app, select a contact and turn On the Drop in button if they have drop-in privileges with you.

- Permission can be granted with Echo Spot by saying "Show my contacts" and using the touch screen to select the contact and toggle on the drop in option, which can be turned off just as easily.

- To drop in on one of your own devices, say something like, "Drop in on my living room Echo Spot".

- The names of the devices in your home can be changed in the Settings on the Alexa App.

There's a video with complete Drop in details here: www.amzn.to/2vJs26V

While I've covered the essential details, there is a section on Alexa Calling and Messaging FAQs located here: www.amzn.to/2xy8nJ1

13: Alexa & Echo Spot: Your Perfect Fit — Settings

For any voice command you read in this chapter be sure to use your wake word ("Alexa", "Amazon", etc) first.

The Settings section is where you control how the Alexa App and Echo Spot function to suit your style. Let's walk through the Settings to get familiar with their contents and how you can tailor your Echo Spot's performance. Select **Settings** on the App Menu to be taken to the **Settings Main Page** where we'll get started.

Devices

The first thing you'll see is a list of the Alexa enabled devices that you own and linked to your Alexa account. The word "Online" appears beneath any device when it is connected to a Wi-Fi network.

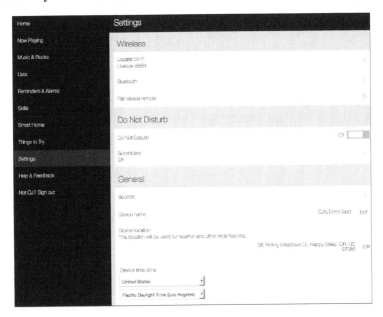

Start by selecting your device from the list, and you'll be taken to a page for basic setup, organization and information. So these are the settings for your particular device:

Do Not Disturb: This feature keeps Echo Spot quiet including preventing incoming Calls, Messages, Drop-ins or Notifications.

At any time, say, "Do not disturb," Alexa will say, "I won't disturb you," or similar, and the screen will darken until you use the wake word again. Saying, "Turn off your screen" works too.

Scheduled Off: Do Not Disturb is programmable using this feature. Here's how:

- On the Alexa App, select the Scheduled box to open Scheduled Do Not Disturb.

- Once you've used this Setting, the time set for Do Not Disturb to Start and End will appear.

- Toggle On the Scheduled button, and if you want to change the times listed, choose Edit at the bottom to Change/Save new times or Cancel to keep them as is.

Sounds: This is where you customize what sounds your Echo Spot makes, when it makes them and how loud they are.

- **Alarm, Timer and Notification Volume:** Slide the bar left for lower and right for higher, and Echo Spot will give a tone at the new volume for you to evaluate.

- **Audio:** The explanation of notifications is just around the corner. This allows you to determine whether a tone is given when a notification hits your Notification List. I keep Audio toggled Off unless I'm eagerly awaiting a Notification about a package being sent out for delivery or a message returned (See Calling & Messaging).

- **Custom Sounds/Alarm:** This section was covered earlier in Reminders & Alarms, but in brief, you can select from celebrity-delivered alarm messages and custom sounds. The Default alarm shows initially; if you change it, the new choice is shown in the box.

Device Name: Once you name your Echo Spot and other Echo devices on your account, the name will appear on the Settings home page and here:

- Select Edit.
- Change the Name.
- Select Save.

Device Location: I've included my complete address to get the best information about distances to restaurants and businesses near me. You don't have to enter any location, or you can input just a street and/ or zip code:

- Select the Edit button.
- Input or change address information.
- Choose Save or Cancel.

Device Time Zone: To show the correct time on your Echo Spot:

- Select a Region or United States from the top box to see your time zone options.
- Select the time zone you want from the lower box.

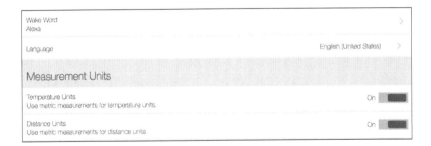

Wake Word: The default wake word is Alexa, but you can change it to Computer, Amazon or Echo. I've tried them all, and Echo is the only viable alternative for me since I often use Amazon and Computer in conversation unrelated to Alexa/Echo Spot. Doing that creates a false "waking" of the device. If you want to change the wake word:

- In the Alexa App go to **Settings > Your Echo Spot > Wake Word**

- Expand the Names box with the down caret.

- Select the name you want.

- Save it, and you'll be taken to the previous page where the Wake Word will appear.

Measurement Units: If you prefer metric units for temperature and distance, toggle the buttons to On.

Device is registered to: CAUTION! Once you set up your Echo Spot, as explained in an earlier section, your name will appear here. The note of caution relates to the option to the right Reset to Factory Defaults. This will deregister your Echo Spot and I'm aware of only two times to do this:

- If you sell or give away the device.

- If you cannot get it to function properly in the future, Amazon recommends deregistering and reregistering it as a last resort.

Deregistering your device can also be done online, for example if you sell your Echo Spot but forget to deregister it first. To deregister any Echo device:

- Go to www.amazon.com/mycd

- Select Your Devices.

- Select the box to the left of the appropriate device.

- In the popup window, select Deregister your device.

- Follow the onscreen prompts.

Accounts

Once you've finished with the device settings above click back to the main Settings page. Below **Devices** you will find **Accounts**. This section gets its name because some of the Settings in it require creating and linking to a third-party account such as Pandora.

Notifications: You might be familiar with Notifications because you get them on your phone, your computer and social media. Alexa uses Notifications in Shopping, Messaging and a few other features:

- Select from this list the type you want to receive and turn the box On or Off as desired.

Music & Media: This section lists the accounts you've linked to Alexa, along with the user ID for the account, and those available to use with Alexa that don't require an account. If you haven't opened an account for these services or haven't yet linked your existing account to the Alexa App, you can do so by selecting any of the music services from the *Music, Video & Books* tab on the App menu. Complete instructions are given in Chapter 5 (page 37). Select any of the Music Services to:

- Unlink the account if you don't use the service or Echo Spot any longer.

- Manage your account Settings by logging into your account on the service's site.

- Manage service-specific Settings such as Enabling Custom Stations on iHeartRadio.

- Learn tips for using the music service.

Select the *Choose Default Music Service* option to choose a default music library and music station. For example, my libraries are Amazon Music and Spotify, and Amazon is my default. When I say, "Play Blake Shelton," Alexa plays music available on Amazon. If I want the music I have in my Spotify collection, I request it — "Play Blake Shelton from Spotify."

Flash Briefing: Most news services create short news summaries hourly or several times per day, in many cases to play on radio. Many of those summaries are available for playing on you Echo Spot whenever you want to hear them. Most are Skills, and we've discussed Skills at length. Together, those summaries you choose make your Flash Briefing.

To create yours:

- Select *Get More Flash Briefing Content.*

- Browse the list, and select the ones you want.

- Enable the Skill.

- Those you choose will be listed here.

- Toggle on those you want to play.

- Choose *Edit Order* to rearrange the order they are played.

- Say, "Play my Flash Briefing," "What's in the news" or similar, and Echo Spot will deliver it.

- Each news service's logo will appear on the Echo Spot screen; some services include video.

- Say, "Skip" or "Next," and Alexa will move on to the next service in the briefing.

- I have 11 services in my briefing, but I often hear the top story from a service and then skip to the next or skip the service altogether.

Sports Update: This feature was covered in the Things to Try chapter (page 87), but here's a summary. The feature allows you to follow professional teams and leagues from North America and Europe plus the football and basketball teams for most major colleges in the US:

- Use the Search your Teams box to find teams you want to follow.

- Click on those teams from the search results.

- They will appear in your list.

- Remove them by selecting the X.

- Say, "Sports update" to hear latest scores and upcoming games for the teams in your list that are currently in season.

Traffic: Also covered in Things to Try, your Traffic feature gives you commute times. Input a "From" location, "To" location and stops in between, if desired. Edit them to change your route, and then ask, "What's my commute?"

Calendars: Alexa can link to calendars from Google, Microsoft and Apple iCloud. Link your calendars, and add items to them with basic requests such as, "Add appointment at 3pm Thursday to my calendar" and hundreds of similar things. See Check and Manage your Calendar in this guide's Things to Try chapter.

Lists: Alexa manages a Shopping List and To-do List for you in the App. You can also link your lists on Alexa to several 3rd party list apps like **AnyList** and **Todoist**:

- Create a free basic or paid premium account on one or more of those sites.
- Select **Settings > Lists.**
- Choose a service and select **Link Account** to connect the account to Alexa.
- Sign into your Amazon account and the list service account.
- Go to the separate app of the chosen service on your phone and tap "Connect with Amazon Echo".
- Sign in.

If you already have an account with one of those services, connecting it with Alexa might make sense. If you don't, it's redundant if you have the Alexa App on your phone.

Voice Purchasing: The details on this topic are covered at length in the Things to Try chapter (page 87) under "Shop Amazon (For Prime Members)". In short, Amazon Prime members with a US address and means of payment stored on Amazon can:

- Enable 1-click shopping on your Amazon account.
- Enable Voice Purchasing here.
- Choose a 4-digit code and require its use with Voice Purchasing.
- Order and reorder Amazon Prime-qualified items with hands-free ease.

Amazon Households: When you create an Amazon Household, you gain four advantages:

- Members share Amazon Prime benefits when Prime Sharing is enabled.

- All digital content can be shared between adults in the household in what Amazon calls a Family Library.

- Select titles can be shared and unshared with children too.

- Payment instruments/methods can be shared with other adults in the Household.

A household can include up to two adults and four children. As we noted earlier, creating and managing an Amazon Household is done through your Amazon account.

On Amazon.com:

1. Hover over **Accounts & Lists** near the top of the page.

2. Select "**Your Account**".

3. In the "Shopping programs and rentals" box, select **Amazon Households** to go to the Manage Your Household / Your Amazon Household Benefits page.

4. Enable Prime Sharing, if desired.

5. Select "Add an Adult," and follow the instructions including providing their login information, so they will have to give it to you or be there with you to type it in.

6. And/or select "Add a Child," Create and Save their Profile, and follow the link to Manage Your Content and Devices to manage the content they can access.

7. Adults and children can be removed just as easily, and you can "leave" a household too.

Leaving and removing can be done in this section of the App too. Select yourself, and choose Leave; select another Household member, and choose Remove. Complete information about households and how to manage yours can be found on this page: www.amazon.com/myh/manage

General

There are two final Settings sections, History and About the Amazon Alexa App.

History: Select this Setting to view your entire voice-interaction history with Alexa. Choose any line to see complete details or to delete the item. To delete all voice recordings and their associated Cards:

* Go to www.amazon.com/mycd

* Select *Your Devices*.

* Select the box to the left of the appropriate device.

* In the popup window, select *Manage voice recordings*, and **Delete** or **Cancel**.

You can also deregister your Echo device or change its name there.

14: Resources Galore — Help & Feedback

This section of the Alexa App provides a wealth of information, though we've already covered much of it and referred to it frequently. When selecting an item from Things to Try, for example, you are usually taken here for the explanation. There are things worth mentioning about this section that haven't been covered yet in this guide.

Alexa and Alexa Device FAQs

These FAQs are difficult to find by navigating through the Help & Feedback section. You can access them on every Card though. Select Learn More in the "Remove Card" box on each Card. They are also found here: www.amzn.to/2xy8nJ1

Let's scroll through Help & Feedback for important areas not yet discussed.

Alexa User Guide

Alexa is the cloud-based AI "brain" for all Echo devices. The Alexa User Guide includes these notable new topics:

Alexa Device Support: Sections of special interest here are:

- **Accessibility Features for Alexa** is an overview of the technology required to make Echo Spot easier to view, hear and communicate with.

- **Differences Between Alexa Devices** is a good source of information if you're interested in adding other devices to your Echo-sphere.

- **Supported Alexa Features** is a companion to the previous section as it lists what main Alexa features are supported by the various devices – which have Bluetooth, Calling & Messaging, alarms & timers, Flash Briefing, Music, Audible, Kindle, etc.

- **Using Multiple Alexa Devices** is must-reading if you do grow your Echo-sphere. There's information about using devices with the same Wake Word, which devices don't require a Wake Word (Amazon Tap, e.g.) and things you can do (like share Music between devices) and things you can't do (like play the same music on more than one device).

- We discussed voice-control of Fire TV in its section in the Video chapter, but the **Use Your Alexa Device to Control Your Fire TV** section in the App offers more detail and will be useful for Fire TV users for linking and controlling content.

- The **Personalize Your Alexa Device** section has all been covered, but this is a handy overview of your options. If you get a free hour, pour a favorite beverage and go through the list to customize what you want Alexa to do for you, something I do about once a month.

- **Differences Between Alexa Voice Remote for Echo and for Fire TV** is a good reminder that the capabilities of these two remotes do not overlap where it counts: The Alexa remote for Echo devices like Echo Spot does not control Fire TV; the Alexa remote for Fire TV doesn't control Echo devices.

Alexa Calling and Messaging: Here is your resource for Calling, Messaging and Drop-In capabilities. The information in this section and its links are comprehensive. You'll find step-by-step instructions to follow for setup and use, if what we discussed earlier isn't clear

Alexa Quick Fixes: This is another section you might find useful. While we've tried to be thorough, and there's nothing new here currently, this section includes information that might have been updated since the publication of this book.

Contact Us

I've had no issues with Echo or Echo Spot that I couldn't solve using the abundance of information found in the Alexa App and on Amazon. com. Because of the good fortune I've had with Alexa and Echo, I haven't emailed or called Customer Service. However, if you have problems and can't find answers, don't hesitate to contact Amazon. Feedback is another issue. I have used the Send Feedback option seven times to date to give Amazon my thoughts on how to improve Alexa/Echo Spot performance. I bring this up to say that Amazon has always been responsive, so if you contact the company with issues, you can expect that a customer service representative will be in touch.

Legal

If you have questions about how Amazon will use your information or what legal parameters there are for using Alexa/Echo Spot, scanning the Legal & Compliance section will provide you with answer

Before You Go

So there you have it! My goal is to provide you with clear, concise information from the perspective of someone that uses Echo Spot and Alexa every day, insight I don't often find when reading pages on Amazon. That's why I wrote this book.

I trust by now you have your Echo Spot up and running and have become familiar with many of its features. Please drop me a line at cjandersentech@gmail.com if you require any further clarification.

And don't forget to sign up for my monthly newsletter; I will keep you up to date with the ever changing features of Alexa.

Get your updates here: www.about.me/cjandersen

30824436R00063

Printed in Great Britain
by Amazon